UnMarried

A M E R I C A

How Singles Are Changing and What It Means for the Church

aBarna**Report**

Published by the Barna Research Group, Ltd.
647 West Broadway • Glendale, CA 91204-1007

© 1993 by the Barna Research Group, Ltd. All rights reserved.

Printed in the United States. ISBN 1-882297-03-2

ISBN 1-882297-03-2

90000

9 781882 297030

Contents

CHAPTER SEVEN:
The Church Ladies
83

CHAPTER EIGHT:
What Happens Next?
97

CHAPTER NINE:
How Should the Church Respond?
105

I N T R O D U C T I O N

On The Outside

*W*hen several single acquaintances of mine learned I was writing a report about unmarrieds, they took issue with the title. "Is that all we are? Just *unmarrieds*?" they asked. "Why are you defining people in terms of marriage when they aren't married in the first place? Call us 'singles.' "

Point taken. Single Americans are not just waiting around to get married; more and more are living fulfilling lives outside of marriage. The Apostle Paul certainly did not treat Corinth's singles as second class citizens.

Then why did we keep the title *Unmarried America?* Ironically, part of the reason is that my critics were right. Life does not begin at marriage, nor does it end at divorce or widowhood. Much of the human experience lies beyond the nucleus of a family. Discovering the behaviors and values associated with non-family experiences, and trying to make some sense of them, is what this report is all about.

The other part of the reason is that my critics were wrong. The family experience is not everything, but it *is* one of the most universal and basic of lifestyles. We remember the family of our youth. All around us are families, both healthy and dysfunctional. Our televisions and newspapers are full of family sagas and tragedies. Ideas about marriage and family influence our thinking and our lifestyles for the rest of our lives.

Marriage is part of the American dream and an indispensable part of many career paths. It is the first step in the process of "settling down." To be President, one must be married. (James Buchanan, the last bachelor, beat the odds in 1857.) To pastor a Protestant church, marriage is virtually a prerequisite (95% are married). And to be the CEO of a Fortune 500 company, one should be married—at least once.

Marriage ranks right up there with birth and death in how profoundly it changes our lives. Until recently, it was also a precondition to experiencing sexuality, childbirth and other fundamental human experiences. It retains a mystique that has lingered even after those experiences have crossed over into the lifestyles of unmarrieds. Marriage is woven into the fabric of society, into our dreams and our anxieties.

Religion and Marriage

Marriage and family have always been of central importance to the Christian church. Christianity has transformed people's notions of marriage since its beginning. For Christians marriage becomes a mystical event where two people become one flesh. The union is even equated with that of Christ and the Church. To Roman Catholic and Eastern Orthodox Christians, it is a sacrament. Despite their excluding marriage from their list of sacraments, many Protestants treat it as if it were still there. Important Christian traditions are family-oriented: infant baptism, religious holidays and feasts and church attendance involve much more than mere individuals. It is through the family that most Christian beliefs and traditions are quietly transmitted while the world of singles rushes past.[1]

Marriage and family issues are a constant preoccupation for most Americans. Ninety-five percent of people who are unmarried expect someday to marry.[2] For both marrieds and never-marrieds, marriage and family issues are a fundamental ministry need and a high priority for churches. Of the changes in lifestyle and attitude that entering and leaving a marriage cause, many involve religion and God. If marriage is central to our secular culture, it is even more central to our religious culture.

Marriage in Decline

Despite all the pronouncements that marriage and traditional families in America are dead, both institutions are still powerful. Political analyst Fred Barnes recently noted that married couples with children comprise a voting bloc of 92 million Americans.[3] But their competition is heating up. Trends, some going back a century, are diminishing the centrality of marriage to our secular culture and changing us as individuals, as families and as a society. Every year a smaller proportion of America is married. Every year the rate of people entering marriages drops, and the rate of people leaving them rises. These shifts are bringing an avalanche of ramifications into our private and public lives. The decline in marriages and the increase in divorces are two important reasons that the gap between our religious culture and our secular culture is growing, and why the church is receding from the lives of so many Americans.

It is imperative that we understand the trends that have already changed us so much, and whose influence will likely continue to grow in coming decades. But it is even more imperative that we understand the people behind the trend lines. Their lives, beliefs and needs all matter. Their lives are filled with experiences unique to their group, and they adopt attitudes and live in ways that are fundamentally different from those of their married counterparts.

Many Unmarried Americans see their lifestyles as largely separate from those of married's. Their concerns are different. They spend their money differently. They think and vote differently. And they react differently to their isolation from the larger married culture. Some do not mind; they are content with their current lifestyles. Other Unmarried Americans feel displaced by mainstream secular and religious culture. They see it as centered on family life, and unable to relate to their world. In order to serve the needs of unmarrieds, let alone work together with them, churches have to understand not just Unmarried Americans' different worlds, but their different attitudes as well.

Marriage is a receding but still powerful force in American society. People who live outside marriage are still shaped by marriage in basic ways. Marriage *does* define and affect Unmarried Americans—even those who have never walked down the aisle themselves.

I hope you find this book as illuminating to read as I have found it to research. And if serving Unmarried America is part of your life's work, as it is part of mine, I hope you find this resource useful as well.

Telford Work
Glendale, CA
September, 1993

N   O   T   E   S

1 Barnes, Fred, "the Family Gap," in *Readers's Digest,* July, 1992, p. 54

2 Bumpass, Larry and James Sweet, National Estimates of Cohabitation: *Cohort Levels and Union Stability*, National Survey of Families and Households Working Paper No. 2 (Madison, Wisconsin: Center for Demography and Ecology, University of Wisconsin, June 1989), p. 3.

3 Barnes, *Reader's Digest,* p. 50

C H A P T E R   O N E

Family Fission

What is happening to the family in America?

"At the resurrection," Jesus said, "people will neither marry nor be given in marriage." (Matthew 22:30, NIV) In more and more of America these days, it is looking a lot like the resurrection. The share of American adults who are not married grew from 27% of the population to 39% between 1965 and 1991.[1] Demographic trends show that Unmarried America will continue to grow; some estimate that by the year 2000 *half* of American adults will be unmarried.

A lot of people need to have their images of Unmarried America brought up to date. Many are simply too used to thinking of people in terms of families, and lump any young, unmarried person into a common "single" category. Unmarried America is disproportionately young; disproportionately black and hispanic; undereducated; poorer; and more distant from the church. Yet unmarried Americans are college graduates as well as high-school dropouts; yuppies as well as homeless people; church pastors as well as alienated agnostics.

Within this block of nearly two in five American adults hides a variety of different marital statuses and living arrangements. In 1991, one-quarter (26%) of American men and nearly one-fifth (19%) of American women had never been married. Almost one-twelfth of men and one-tenth of women were currently divorced or separated.[2] About 4% of Americans over 18 were cohabiting.[3] Seven percent of American adults were widows or widowers. Finally, living with all these adults were 28% of American children—more than one in four.[4] One label, whether it is "single" or "unmarried," could never accurately describe all these

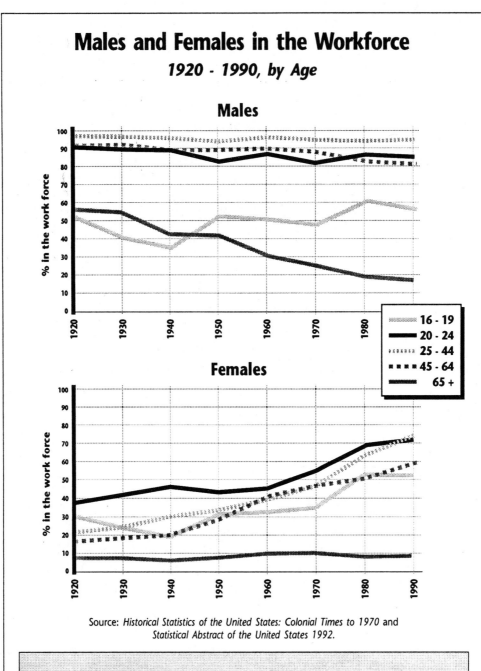

Males and Females in the Workforce
1920 - 1990, by Age

Males

Females

Legend:
- 16 - 19
- 20 - 24
- 25 - 44
- 45 - 64
- 65 +

Source: *Historical Statistics of the United States: Colonial Times to 1970* and *Statistical Abstract of the United States 1992.*

These figures compare the labor force participation rate of men and women of different age groups over the last 100 years. Its most prominent features are the rapid rise in the share of women who work (except women 65 and older) and the gradually shrinking retirement age of men. In 1890, even most men 65 and over continued to work; in 1990, though their numbers and health were far greater, fewer than 20% worked. The share of working men 45-64 years of age is heading downward as well. Boys and girls 16-19 years old were more likely to work in the beginning of the century, dropped out of the workforce in the 1930's and 40's, and have since then returned. The Great Depression may well have been a factor in these changes.

people. Never-married adults, cohabiting couples, divorced adults and widows live radically different lives. They have unique interests, pressures and needs. Though they live side by side, they occupy different social and economic strata.

How Did We Get Here?

A proper understanding of the strange story of the American family in the past few decades begins with economic change. The incredible economic growth of the twentieth century has constantly wrenched Americans from one way of life to another. Advances in technology freed wives from much of their daily, manual work and sped the country's transformation from a rural to an urban and finally a suburban society. Economic change pushed people in and out of the workforce and led to earlier and earlier retirement ages for men. Immigration and assimilation, World Wars I and II, the New Deal and the Baby Boom, to name only a few events, all shaped America and the American family. These forces are among those responsible for giving us the "Father Knows Best" families of the '50s.

A new set of forces has been helping to break up the American family since the '60s. Further technological change made the two-earner family a possibility for many, and the end of the unparalleled era of economic expansion that lasted from World War II until 1973 made it a common lifestyle for people struggling to fulfill the American Dream for themselves and their children.

Alongside these economic trends came powerful and unprecedented social trends as well: the sexual revolution, the fertility decline among American women and the "divorce revolution."[5] Now we face a present and a future America where one-quarter of all children are born outside marriage, where marriages are as likely to be ended by divorce as by death, and where some view the very institution of marriage as outdated.

Persistent Trends

Most analyses of American society use the 1950s or '60s as a baseline. But in many ways, the '50s and '60s turn out to be exceptional, not normal, years. For instance, the share of Americans who were married in 1950 was much higher than in either 1890 or 1990. So was the rate of economic growth—and even the growth in the numbers of divorced people!

Rates of Growth in Marrieds, Never-marrieds, Divorced and Widowed People

Percentage Growth Rate for Each Marital Status

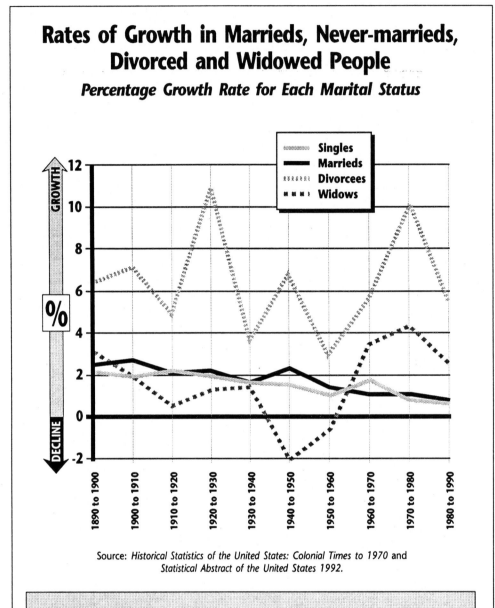

Source: *Historical Statistics of the United States: Colonial Times to 1970* and
Statistical Abstract of the United States 1992.

This chart records and compares the rates of growth in the numbers of never-marrieds, marrieds, divorced people and widowed people. Any point above the baseline indicates increasing numbers over the decade, while any point below the baseline indicates decline. It reveals some important trends:

- Divorce was growing long before the "divorce revolution" of the 1970's. The number of divorced people has been growing only somewhat more quickly than it has over the last century. In the 1920's the divorce rate actually grew faster than it did in the 1970's; but the trend was much less noticeable because in the 20's the numbers of divorced people were much smaller than at the beginning of the 1970's. The rate of growth slowed dramatically between the 1970's and the 1980's.

- The 1940's and 50's, a time many people consider normal, were actually

continued on next page...

The accompanying chart shows how far back some trends actually go. It displays *rates* of growth—rather like a graph of interest rates—and yields some surprising information.

For instance, for the last century the number of divorced Americans has been growing faster than the number of married Americans. Growth has hovered around the 7% level, compared to less than 2% growth in the number of marrieds. Given rates like these, the coming of the "divorce revolution" was only a matter of time.

On the other hand, the number of never-marrieds grew slowly during the first half of the century, actually *declined* in the 1940's and '50s and boomed in the '60s, '70s and '80s. It is here that we see the number of never-marrieds rise from an unusually low base in the 1950s to an unusually high level in the '60s and '70s. In the 1980s the growth rate slowed as Baby Boomers married and the less massive Baby Buster generation came of age; yet the number of never-marrieds is still increasing at almost four times the rate of the number of marrieds.

Another trend is more subtle but no less noteworthy. The growth rate in married Americans has slowed more or less consistently since 1900 (except during the Baby Boom years, a truly exceptional era for marriages as well as for births). Since the '60s the numbers of married Americans have grown at only a crawl. Once again, given these growth rates, the rise of Unmarried America was only a

---

continued from previous page...

exceptional decades. The number of never-marrieds actually shrank in the 1940's and 1950's, and the number of marrieds grew unusually quickly. (Some of the decline can be attributed to deaths in World War II, and some can be attributed to the increase in married people during the same period.) Yet in these decades, the numbers of divorced people were growing more rapidly than any other marital group.

- Following this unusual period came a dramatic rise in the numbers of never-marrieds, a rise in the divorce rate and a slowdown in the growth of married people. The greatest change in growth rates over the last thirty years has not been in divorced people, nor even married people, but in never-married people. As Baby Boomers became adults, their numbers swelled the ranks of never-marrieds. The change looks even more dramatic compared to the 1940's and 1950's. At no other time this century did never-married adults increase at a faster rate than married adults.

- Marriage rates have slowly been stagnating. The number of marrieds has actually grown throughout this era and continues to do so today. But the rate of growth has shrunk more or less steadily since 1900, with the sole exception of the 1940's. The high rates of growth both of never-married people and of divorced people stand in marked contrast to this plateauing of married adults. If divorced and never-married adults continue to increase more quickly than married adults, it is inevitable that *Unmarried America* will become an ever-growing part of America.

matter of time—even had the Baby Boom era and the revolutions of the '60s never happened.[6]

Whether we approve of the trends or not, they will not vanish overnight. There is no going back to a time when wives performed household chores all day and birth control was unthinkable, much less unavailable. Whatever lies in America's future, it is not our social or our economic past.

Growing Numbers of Niches

Who are the people who make up the growing ranks of Unmarried America? First of all, they are a lot more than just "singles." Once upon a time, when the Baby Boom generation was growing up and leaving home, Unmarried America looked a lot like Never-Married America. But now Baby Boomers, and Baby Busters too, are settling down in new ways—such as, getting divorced, staying single, living together, and moving back in with their parents. The "unmarried" category now encompasses "never-married," "cohabiting" or living together, "cohabiting parent," "single parent," "divorced," "separated," and "widowed."

A large church in the Los Angeles area offers a whole range of Sunday school classes that revolve around marriage: a class for engaged couples, a special seminar that is mandatory for anyone who intends to marry at the church, a newly-marrieds class, a new-parents class and so on. Recently, though, the variety of classes has begun to grow on the unmarried side as well. The never-married class was recently augmented by a "single again" class for divorced people and widows. This church, like many others, has begun to respond to the unique needs of some of society's emerging subgroups. Besides young never-married people who are out of school and on their own, there are "single" elderly widows, "single" unmarried mothers, "single" couples who live together and plan to be married soon and "single" fortysomething divorced people. The "single" lifestyle just is not a one-size-fits-all reality.

Time for a Change

Unmarried America's incredible diversity owes itself to one basic social phenomenon: as people in our society age, their lifestyles and interests change dramatically. Specific experiences, like marriage, divorce or the arrival of children, cause some of these changes. Others are the result of physical limitations due to aging, or new economic and social realities that emerge as people age.

You can see these processes at work when looking at the lifestyles of marrieds and unmarrieds of various ages. For instance:

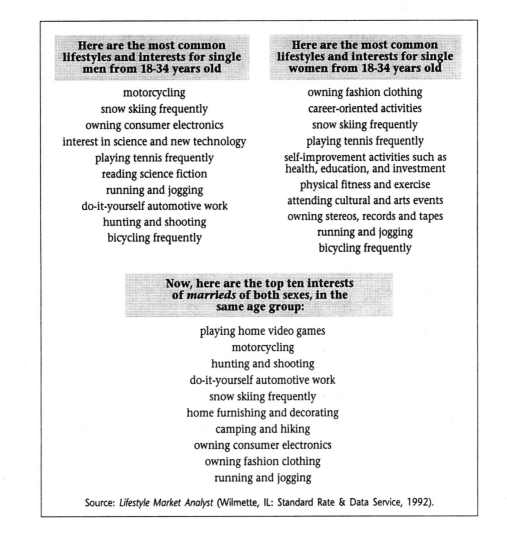

Here are the most common lifestyles and interests for single men from 18-34 years old

motorcycling
snow skiing frequently
owning consumer electronics
interest in science and new technology
playing tennis frequently
reading science fiction
running and jogging
do-it-yourself automotive work
hunting and shooting
bicycling frequently

Here are the most common lifestyles and interests for single women from 18-34 years old

owning fashion clothing
career-oriented activities
snow skiing frequently
playing tennis frequently
self-improvement activities such as health, education, and investment
physical fitness and exercise
attending cultural and arts events
owning stereos, records and tapes
running and jogging
bicycling frequently

Now, here are the top ten interests of *marrieds* of both sexes, in the same age group:

playing home video games
motorcycling
hunting and shooting
do-it-yourself automotive work
snow skiing frequently
home furnishing and decorating
camping and hiking
owning consumer electronics
owning fashion clothing
running and jogging

Source: *Lifestyle Market Analyst* (Wilmette, IL: Standard Rate & Data Service, 1992).

Career-oriented activities, tennis, self-improvement, cultural and arts events, music, bicycling and sci fi begin at the top of unmarrieds' lists. After marriage, these endeavors are replaced by home video games, home furnishing and decorating, camping and hiking. People with shiny new rings on their fingers also have shiny new sets of priorities.

A complicating factor is that the older singles are from a different generation. Each group of singles has inherited a different world and has been brought up differently, and its attitudes reflect its unique origins.[8]

But along with marriage and generational differences, age also changes the lives of singles. Single men between 35 and 44 years old are more worried about boating and money-making opportunities than about skiing and tennis. Single women in this age group go for fine art and antiques, health foods and vitamins, dieting and weight control, home decorating, wine and owning cats, rather than for skiing, tennis, exercise, music, running and bicycling.

The lesson here is not that older people will not go on a ski retreat for "singles." It is that these different people lead very different lives. Their concerns change; their financial pictures change; their emotional needs change. By the time unmarrieds are over 65, they are more likely to be involved with grandchildren, crossword puzzles, needlework and knitting, sewing, walking for health, veterans benefits, politics, health foods and vitamins and book reading. Consequently, ministry to "singles" must reflect these different life stages and perspectives.

If unmarried seniors come to your ski retreat, they will be showing pictures of their grandchildren, not their Harleys. When they talk about money, they are thinking in terms of mortgage payments, not rent: two-thirds of them own their homes, versus only one-quarter of single 18- to 34-year-olds. Singles over 65 may be an extreme example; but they are just the end-result of a gradual process of change that affects people throughout their lives.

Who Are the Bible Readers?

Spiritual priorities change along with other lifestyle priorities. If you decide to hold a Bible study at your ski retreat, expect the older people to be a lot better prepared, and the single parents to dominate the discussion. Fewer than 11% of single adults under 35 years old list Bible or devotional reading as interests; 23% of singles over 65 living without children do. And over one-third—36%—of all unmarrieds with children at home list Bible or devotional reading as interests.

Though perhaps not as much as Little League and PTAs, participation in the life of a church is a family thing. On the whole, Unmarried America is less involved in organized religion than are married adults and their offspring. But each group's degree of involvement differs. At one extreme, many young unmarrieds have little understanding of Christianity and fail to see the point of church. At the other, widows are relatively familiar with Christianity and consider churches responsive to their needs.

Many surveys and studies show a tendency for people to become more involved in churches as they become more involved in family life. Many pastors have watched the Baby Boomers grow up and heaved sighs of relief, knowing that marrieds and parents were more likely to come back to church. The reasons for their change of heart are well known: many want to give their children a religious education, even if the parents themselves had a miserable time in church when they were children. New families settle down and begin their lives of responsibility, and middle-agers begin to grapple with their mortality and persistent questions about the meaning of life.

But American society did not spring back to its pre-Baby Boom shape. Instead, it became something altogether new. With less of America married than ever, and with growing numbers of Americans rejecting the very idea of the two-parent family, banking on returning Boomers seems a less and less viable strategy for churches that want to be revitalized. Time is *not* on their side. Every day brings more single parents, more widows, more cohabiters, more divorced adults for churches to care for. As Unmarried America grows, the challenge to the Church grows along with it.

Where Do Unmarrieds Live?

Add geography to age, generation, marital and parental status as a factor that differentiates Unmarried America from Married America. Singles are unevenly distributed throughout the country. They are plentiful in certain towns and relatively scarce in most rural communities. Domestic immigration and emigration account for some of the age diversity: students move to college towns, recent graduates and working-age families move out of depressed areas (leaving their parents there) and into emerging economic centers, and retirees move to favorable climates like Florida and Arizona. Other factors include cities' racial makeup and the local cost of living.

College towns like Lafayette, Indiana; Gainesville, Florida; Charlottesville, Virginia and Austin, Texas have large contingents of unmarrieds between 18 and 34. Unmarrieds between 35 and 44, on the other hand, tend to be concentrated in larger communities. Las Vegas, New York, Washington D.C. and Los Angeles all have an above-average proportion of middle-aged unmarrieds. And Unmarried

Americans approaching their retirement years—45 to 64 years old—are concentrated in cities like New York, Miami, Baltimore, Palm Springs and Philadelphia.

Unmarrieds with children under 18 living at home are found in still different areas: one-eighth (13%) of the households in the Greenwood-Greenville area of Mississippi are headed by singles with children in the home—nearly double the proportion for America as a whole! Other communities with high concentrations of single parents are Brownsville, Texas; Bakersfield, California; El Paso, Texas and Jackson, Mississippi.

These concentrations present opportunities to churches who want to serve their unique needs. Churches in college towns commonly target ministries to undergraduates. But churches in locations with large proportions of unmarried adults enjoy similar, if less obvious, opportunities to minister to the needy people who surround them.

Table 1-1
Top Ten Communities With The Greatest Share of Unmarried Households

"Single Male, 18-34 Years Old":	% of households:
Lafayette, IN	15%
Gainesville, FL	15
Charlottesville, VA	14
Austin, TX	13
Flagstaff, AZ	12
Waco-Temple-Bryan, TX	12
Mankato, MN	11
Denver, CO	11
Baton Rouge, LA	11
Tuscaloosa, AL	11
national average	***8***

"Single Female, 18-34 Years Old"	
Charlottesville, VA	11
Gainesville, FL	11
Austin, TX	9
Lafayette, IN	9
Denver, CO	9
Flagstaff, AZ	9
Washington, DC	8
Madison, WI	8

Continued on next page →

Lansing, MI 8
Tallahassee-Thomasville, FL 8
national average **6**

"Single Male, 35-44 Years Old"

Las Vegas, NV 6
Reno, NV 5
San Francisco-Oakland-San Jose, CA 5
Washington, DC 5
Flagstaff, AZ 5
Los Angeles, CA 5
Salinas-Monterey, CA 5
Baltimore, MD 5
Greenville-New Bern-Wash, NC 5
New York, NY 5
national average **4**

"Single Female, 35-44 Years Old"

McAllen-Brownsville, TX 6
New York, NY 6
Florence-Myrtle Beach, SC 6
Washington, DC 6
New Orleans, LA 5
Los Angeles, CA 5
San Francisco-Oakland-San Jose, CA 5
El Paso, TX 5
Boston, MA 5
Chicago, IL 5
national average **4**

"Single, 45-64 Years Old, No Child at Home"

New York, NY 10
Miami-Ft. Lauderdale, FL 10
Baltimore, MD 9
Salisbury, MD 9
Palm Springs, CA 9
Philadelphia, PA 9
San Francisco-Oakland-San Jose, CA 9
Santa Barbara-Santa Maria-San Luis Obispo, CA 9
Buffalo, NY 9
Los Angeles, CA 9
national average **8**

"Single, 65+ Years Old, No Child at Home"

Ottumwa-Kirksville, IA-MO 14
Sarasota, FL 14
Wilkes-Barre-Scranton, PA 13

Continued on next page →

Greenwood-Greenville, MS 13
Wheeling-Steubenville, WV-OH 13
Quincy-Hannibal, IL-MO 13
St. Joseph, MO 13
Clarksburg-Weston, WV 13
Utica, NY 13
Marquette, MI 13
national average 9

Single, Any Child at Home:
Greenwood-Greenville, MS 13
McAllen-Brownsville, TX 9
Bakersfield, CA 9
El Paso, TX 9
Albany, GA 9
Jackson, MS 9
New Orleans, LA 9
El Centro-Yuma, CA-AZ 9
Baton Rouge, LA 9
Macon, GA 9
national average 6

Source: *Lifestyle Market Analyst* (Wilmette, Illinois: Standard Rate & Data Service, 1992).

That singles are more or less concentrated in certain areas and have somewhat similar interests points up the fact that each of these demographic groups lives, to an extent, in a culture of its own. America is diversifying maritally just as it is socially, racially and culturally. Increasingly, contact between one unmarried group and another, or between married and unmarried groups, is a cross-cultural experience. Each shares in the common American culture in many ways, but perceives the rest of America only through its own perspective.

Churches send missionaries overseas knowing that they must be trained to understand the people they will be living with, to speak the language, and to be comfortable operating in a foreign culture. How well have your church members been trained to understand the many groups that comprise Unmarried America?

N O T E S

1 U.S. Bureau of the Census, *Statistical Abstract of the United States 1992* (Washington, DC: U.S. Government Printing Office, 1993), p. 44.

2 Ibid., pp. 44-45.

3 Bumpass, Larry and James Sweet, *National Estimates of Cohabitation: Cohort Levels and Union Stability*, National Survey of Families and Households Working Paper No. 2 (Madison, Wisconsin: Center for Demography and Ecology, University of Wisconsin, June 1989), p. 6.

4 Ibid., p. 55.

5 Popenoe, David, "Flight from the Nuclear Family: Trends of the Past Three Decades," *Public Perspective* (March-April 1991).

6 *Historical Statistics of the United States: Colonial Times to 1970* (White Plains, New York: Kraus International Publications, 1989), p. 20 and *Statistical Abstract of the United States 1992*, p. 44.

7 This information comes from the 1992 edition of the *Lifestyle Market Analyst* (Wilmette, Illinois: Standard Rate & Data Service, 1992).

8 For more information differentiating Baby Boomers from Baby Busters, see Barna, George, *The Invisible Generation: Baby Busters* (Glendale, California: Barna Research Group, Ltd., 1992).

C H A P T E R T W O

The Subcultures of Unmarried Americans

*F*or our purposes, the millions of Unmarried Americans fall roughly into several distinct groups: never-marrieds, unmarrieds who live together, divorced adults, single parents and widows. Within these boundaries, unmarrieds have a unique identity and some surprising traits. Much of the rest of this report is devoted to discussing these identities and anomalies as well as what they mean for the church.

Never-Marrieds

When most people say "single," they mean "never married." This group makes up six-tenths of Unmarried America.[1] Their lives are portrayed as independent, career-driven, cosmopolitan and wild (though "wild" in the '90s is not what it used to be). They live their lives in the ever-growing gap between school and marriage.

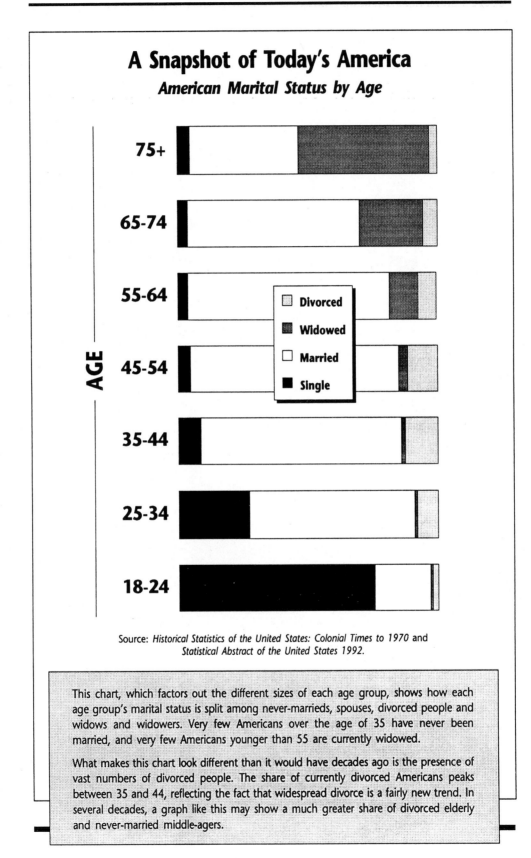

A Snapshot of Today's America
American Marital Status by Age

AGE

75+

65-74

55-64

- Divorced
- Widowed
- Married
- Single

45-54

35-44

25-34

18-24

Source: *Historical Statistics of the United States: Colonial Times to 1970* and
Statistical Abstract of the United States 1992.

This chart, which factors out the different sizes of each age group, shows how each age group's marital status is split among never-marrieds, spouses, divorced people and widows and widowers. Very few Americans over the age of 35 have never been married, and very few Americans younger than 55 are currently widowed.

What makes this chart look different than it would have decades ago is the presence of vast numbers of divorced people. The share of currently divorced Americans peaks between 35 and 44, reflecting the fact that widespread divorce is a fairly new trend. In several decades, a graph like this may show a much greater share of divorced elderly and never-married middle-agers.

Many spend the lion's share of their time establishing their careers and finances, waiting for and working toward the transformation that marriage will eventually bring. They own small cars, rent small apartments and, despite the glamorous image, generally squeak by on small budgets. An increasing number live with their parents.

Most of America's 42 million never-marrieds fit this profile, which at first looks much like the profile of a never-married American living in the '50s. But a closer look reveals differences that have developed over the past few decades. First of all, most never-marrieds are sexually active. Sex—albeit "safe" sex—is an accepted way of life for most never-marrieds. It carries little of its former social stigma. Second, fewer never-marrieds are seeking marriage. For many reasons—more years in school, changing economies and greater personal freedoms—this group is waiting longer to marry than its parents did. In fact, a growing minority are foregoing marriage altogether.

The latter two trends may be reversed in coming years due to demographic or economic change; to conclude that they represent the inexorable wave of the future would be a mistake. About 90% of Americans will eventually marry.[2] Nevertheless, the increased prevalence of premarital sexual activity is a trend of a much different magnitude. There is little reason to expect current sexual attitudes to reverse themselves anytime soon.

One feature of the never-married lifestyle—religion—is most notable for its relative absence. A substantial minority of never-marrieds hold strong religious views and are involved in churches, so it is unfair to call all never-marrieds "unchurched" or "irreligious." Nevertheless, they are the least churched part of Unmarried America. In no other unmarried subgroup, and certainly not among marrieds, is participation in organized religion such a remote experience. Never-marrieds see churches as catering to the needs of married people and their children. Never-marrieds pray less, talk about their faith less, go to church less and read the Bible less than even other unmarrieds.

Never-marrieds, in general, are not hostile to religion, even organized religion. They are just uninterested. As more and more churches seek to strengthen their presence in the lives of unmarried people, they will find this fast-growing group the hardest nut to crack.

Cohabiters: Living Together Without Marrying

Earlier we mentioned that more and more never-marrieds are foregoing marriage altogether. What many are foregoing marriage in favor of is cohabitation—living together. Almost one in four Americans has cohabited at some point in his or her life, and nearly half of all people who married recently had cohabited before-hand.[3] Living together is an increasingly common and socially acceptable lifestyle in its own right.

The image of cohabiting carries its own set of stereotypes which reflect the glamorous side of cohabitation and the fact that the arrangement is still a fairly new lifestyle. But the label hides a variety of lifestyles. As a whole, cohabiters are as diverse as never-marrieds and seem to cohabit for several different reasons: as an interim step leading to marriage, as a living arrangement that is an alternative to marriage, and as a time of "testing" a relationship before engagement. Various demographic groups practice different "types" of cohabitation, and even see each type differently in terms of morality. Within the different groups and types of cohabitation are nuances and values that reveal much of Unmarried America's complex reaction to marriage's changing character and role in society.

But one thing is clear from the numbers: cohabitation is catching on. Its stigma is fading, just as the stigmas of divorce and premarital sex have faded. In the 1990's, marriage is no longer the only socially acceptable game in town.

Divorce and Its Casualties

While marriage's front door has been closing slowly, its back door has been widening fast. Thirty years ago, 35 in 1,000 Americans were divorced. Now the figure is 148 in 1,000—*four times* its previous size. Today, nearly 16 million Americans (one in seven adults) are currently divorced.[4]

Only those who watch too much television would romanticize the lives of divorced people. The first year after their marriages end is chaotic and lonely. Their income and expenses change radically. Many are thrown from the "couples" lifestyle back into single life. Many newly divorced people find the change liberating at first, but the euphoria usually soon gives way to loneliness and discouragement.

Divorced people's lives settle down after the first year, but they remain deeply affected by the experience. Typically, divorced adults are extremely needy, yet extraordinarily giving at the same time. Many are supporting children against longer odds than they had bargained for, around full-time work schedules and reduced budgets. They find marriage alluring and important to family stability, but defend their ability to raise their children alone. Divorced people remain cynical about the future of others' marriages and see instability as a permanent part of American society. Their attitudes in life reflect both the pain and pleasure of their relationships.

The experience of divorce changes its victims' attitudes towards marriage, family, public institutions and God. Perhaps because of their greater needs, divorced people tend to be more religious than average. At the same time, their suspicion of organizations crosses over into suspicion of the Church. Though they are more likely than average to be born again in their beliefs, they practice "private" religion. They see Christianity, not a local church, as relevant to their lives.

Though they share a common experience—the destruction of their families—the lifestyles of divorced adults vary dramatically. Some become introverted. Many older divorced people live more like widows than singles. Others resume dating. Still others adopt a fast-lane, promiscuous lifestyle. Many concentrate on raising their families. And, before remarrying, two-thirds of divorced people cohabit.[5]

Once again, the label masks the diversity within the category. "Divorced people" are an extremely varied group who nevertheless share a common name, a common experience and a worldview that remains fundamentally shaped by that reality.

Single Parents

It is hard to believe that once upon a time the ideas of family, sex and childbirth were intricately related in people's minds. Our ancestors could not even conceive of an America where a married couple "decides" when they want to begin having children. That America arrived a few decades ago. With the advent of effective and inexpensive contraception, sex and childbirth no longer went hand in hand. Nor did sex and family go together, as a flip through the newspaper or television channels will quickly confirm.

Now, the last side of the triangle, family and childbirth, is collapsing as well. Variety reigns in the parental world just as it does everywhere in America. Today's single parents may be never-married and living with their parents, as many teenage mothers are. They may be cohabiting in arrangements that more closely resemble traditional families than single-parent families, or they may be divorced people who had children while they were still married.

Both time and money are in short supply for single parents. The median income of two-parent families in 1991 was $39,996. For female-headed households with no husband present, the median income was less than half ($18,069)[6] of the traditional family's earnings. Single-parent families are overwhelmingly more likely to live under the already-too-low poverty level. Child support payments do not even begin to fill in the gap.

The "cycle of poverty" hits these people hard. Single-parent families are not only poor, but also less educated. Their children are more likely to go to jail. Their energy is exhausted not in improving, but merely in maintaining their lives.

In their attitudes on life and the Church, single parents are much closer to married parents than to divorced adults or unmarrieds without kids. The young lives they support make them more aware of God and more concerned with helping others and raising their children in a spiritual environment. At the same time, single parents lack the adult companionship that most marrieds, and even many never-marrieds, take for granted. Though they may have been spared the shock of divorce, they nevertheless feel the pressures of the single family life.

Widows and Widowers

What could possibly be new about widows? Plenty.

Widowhood in America is changing. In fact, a quick look back through recent history shows that widowhood has not recently *begun to change* so much as it has been *continuing to change*. In the early twentieth century, widows and widowers, not divorced people, headed most single-parent families. Because of this century's economic and medical advances, both men and women live longer than they used to. In fact, during the first half of the century, declines in early deaths among parents actually offset the increasing divorce rate and kept the share of children growing up in single-parent households constant.

Today, only 2% of children live with one widowed parent. But widows' share of America's population has remained relatively constant throughout the century.[7] As a result, a widow is much more likely to be the last bird in the nest.

Most of America's nearly 16 million widows[8] still struggle to live on tiny budgets funded by Social Security checks, inadequate pensions and inflation-eroded savings. Widows are more likely to live in rural than urban settings. More than 80% do not work.[9]

But today's type of widowhood has advantages over its predecessors. Fewer modern-day widows have to take on the task of raising children. And in part because of Social Security, elderly poverty is much decreased by the standards of even a few decades ago. Today's widows have more money to spend on leisure. If the Golden Years are still overly romanticized, they are a much more pleasant time of life for most Americans than they once were.

Many widows are elderly, and therefore come from America's most staunchly traditional age group. Having developed their attitudes and values in an era when divorce was less acceptable, older widows and their married contemporaries represent a time gone by in many ways. Their experiences, values, beliefs and the stability of their marriages have left widows with more traditional views than those of their unmarried counterparts. They are more likely to describe themselves as conservative and to be influenced by biblical teaching on family, morality and sex than their children are. They are more likely to be involved in their communities and much more likely to be involved in a church than are other groups.

It remains to be seen whether the next generation's senior citizens will be as traditional as today's. Studies repeatedly show the tendency for people to become more conservative as they age. But more conservative than what? Future widows, especially Baby Boomer widows, will have more secular backgrounds and less past church involvement, shallower Bible knowledge and lower respect for traditional church approaches. More of their friends will be divorced men and women who never remarried and people who never married in the first place. Graying Boomers will continue to leave a wake of a changed social landscape, a different American Church and a new set of needs.

Unmarried America Close Up

The aforementioned groups are the largest segments of Unmarried America. Their differences present a challenge for any church that wants to "reach" its "community," because unmarrieds' tastes, attitudes, backgrounds and lifestyles reveal not one but many superimposed communities.

Churches are trying a variety of approaches to solve the problem of reaching unmarrieds. Many take the view that people will be attracted to traditional services or solid teaching regardless of cultural influences or personal preferences. Others try to offer services or outreaches that these groups will find more culturally familiar and more relevant to their felt needs. In between the two poles, a vast number of churches are trying to find some sort of "middle ground" between tradition and innovation.

Regardless of the approach a church chooses, familiarity with the people in the pews is an absolute imperative. What follows is an in-depth look at each of these groups, revealing what makes what makes them "tick."

N   O   T   E   S

1   U.S. Bureau of the Census, *Singleness in America: Bureau of the Census Statistical Brief* (Washington, DC: U.S. Government Printing Office, 1989).

2   Ibid.

3   Bumpass, Larry and James Sweet, *Young Adults' Views of Marriage, Cohabitation, and Family*, National Survey of Families and Households Working Paper No. 33 (Madison, Wisconsin: Center for Demography and Ecology, University of Wisconsin), p. 1.

4   *Statistical Abstract of the United States 1992*, p. 44.

5   Thomson, Elizabeth and Ugo Colella, *Cohabitation and Marital Stability: Quality or Commitment?* National Survey of Families and Households Working Paper No. 23, (Madison, Wisconsin: Center for Demography and Ecology, University of Wisconsin, January 1991), p. 5.

6   *Statistical Abstract 1992*, p. 446.

7   *Historical Statistics of the United States, Colonial Times to 1970* (White Plains, New York: Kraus International Publications, 1989), pp. 20-21, and *Statistical Abstract 1992* p. 44.

8   *Statistical Abstract 1992* p. 43.

9   Barna Research Group, Ltd., Family in America survey (Glendale, California: Barna Research Group, Ltd 1992).

C H A P T E R   T H R E E

Never-Marrieds

*T*he ascendency of the "singles culture" in the last few decades results from a combination of trends. The Baby Boom is commonly pointed to as the primary cause of this transformation. But other forces have certainly played a part, and the phenomenon badly needs to be put into a historical perspective that considers what life was like before the "Leave It To Beaver" era.

The average ages of brides and grooms at the turn of the century actually did not look much different than they do today.[1] But after World War II, Americans began to marry earlier. The downward trend "peaked" in the '50s when the average man was under age 23 when he married, and the average woman under 21. Since then, average ages have crept upward until in 1991 men who married waited until age 26, women until nearly 24, to tie the knot. We tend to see the 1950's as the rule, when in reality it was quite an exception!

These millions of early-marrying Americans helped spawn the Baby Boom, which in turn became a growing tide of young singles that appeared in the 1970's. Their massive numbers reversed the momentum, turning it away from marriage. Yet not only did these people wait longer to marry, but fewer of them chose to marry at all, for reasons ranging from emerging careerism among women to a philosophical aversion to the very idea of the lifelong commitment that marriage represents.

The combination of demographic changes, postponed weddings and forgone marriages rapidly increased the size of never-married America in the last two decades, from 16% of the adult population in 1970 to 23% in 1991. One man in four has never been married, compared to one woman in five. Today 21% of white adults are never-married, compared with 37% of black adults.[2]

Currently, never-marrieds are among the most visible groups in America. Television shows like "Melrose Place" seek to tantalize us with images of the carefree lives of the hip and unhitched. Advertisers are turning to the newly-independent Baby Busters as Baby Boomers pour money into their mortgages—

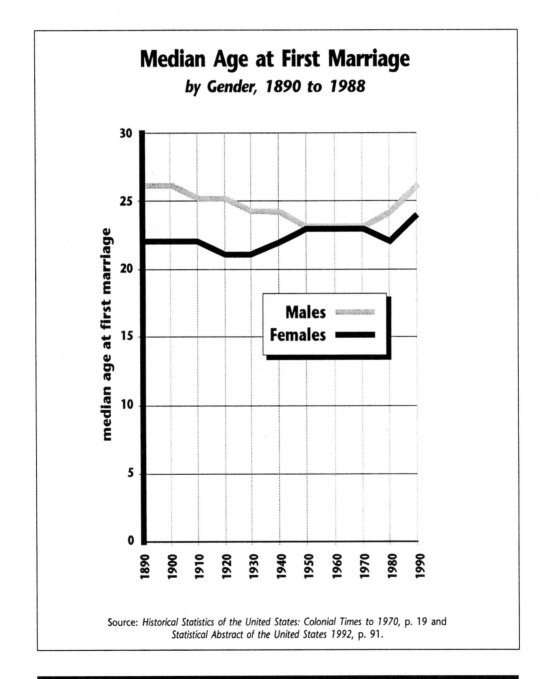

Median Age at First Marriage
by Gender, 1890 to 1988

Source: *Historical Statistics of the United States: Colonial Times to 1970*, p. 19 and *Statistical Abstract of the United States 1992*, p. 91.

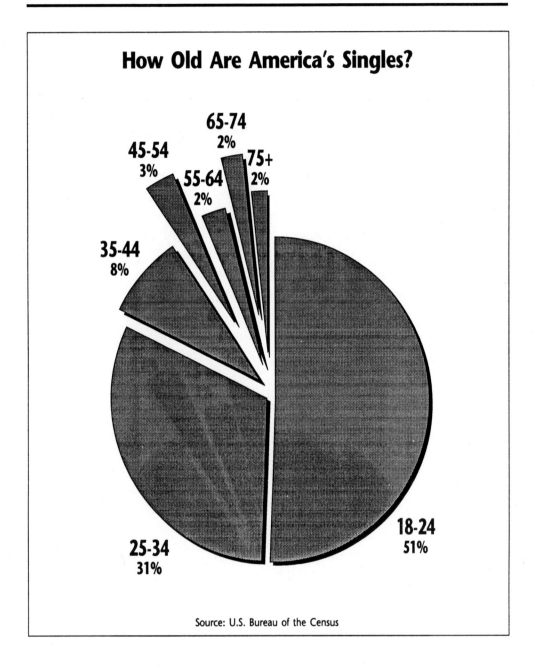

How Old Are America's Singles?

65-74
2%

45-54
3%

55-64
2%

75+
2%

35-44
8%

18-24
51%

25-34
31%

Source: U.S. Bureau of the Census

despite the fact that never-marrieds watch less television than either marrieds or divorced people.[3] Never-marrieds' visibility lends them an influence beyond their numbers that is leaving a lasting effect on the country.

This influential group of people is overwhelmingly suburban and urban. Eighty percent of never-marrieds say they are employed full- or part-time, a ratio that is higher than for any other category. They tend to be poorer than marrieds, but are much better off financially than divorced or widowed Americans. Six in ten have gone to college, making never-marrieds better educated than any other group.[4]

Haves, But More Have-Nots

In order to portray an entire American subculture, we have to generalize; at the same time, it is impossible to confine ourselves to only one portrait. The same character emerges when looking at never-marrieds that we see with every other subgroup within Unmarried America: *diversity*. Never-marrieds are a polarized group of people. Even though their income and net worth are lower than that of marrieds' on average, never-marrieds make up nearly half of the people earning over $100,000 a year. Though never-marrieds are disproportionately black and hispanic, they are also disproportionately suburban. Never-marrieds are very well educated as a whole, but they are also unusually likely to engage in crimes of violence and theft. More than half of all state prison inmates have never been married.

Never-marrieds respond to economic signals in unique ways. Asked recently how they intended to compensate for the currently weak economy, never-marrieds were less likely than others to curb their spending on entertainment, to eat out less often and to reduce their driving. At the same time, they were more likely to buy more items on credit and to try to move to less expensive housing.[5] These decisions reflect never-marrieds' own special sets of priorities and expenses.

The range of financial priorities reflects the diversity within this group. At one end of the social scale, never-marrieds have more leisure time and more discretionary income to spend on leisure activities. This helps explain their penchant for skiing, motorcycle riding, health clubs and entertainment. It also helps explain never-marrieds' packed schedules in spite of their sparse commitments.

Toward the middle of the social scale, being unmarried is more of a financial burden. Nearly one-quarter of never-marrieds earn less than $20,000 a year. In a world where husbands and wives increasingly combine incomes, these people are at a real disadvantage. They compete with married couples for the same apartments and houses. They are less able to split rents, food and utility bills. Many bear the expense of dating. In some cities their auto insurance is astronomical. Many unmarrieds—even middle-class unmarrieds—constantly struggle to make ends meet and race to keep up with the ever-rising cost of living.

Living with roommates is one traditional way for never-marrieds to economize on time as well as money. They team up not just into twos, but also into threes and fours to share apartments, condos or small houses. Some even continue to share housing with their roommates after they have married.

Some traditional living arrangements are making a comeback. "Every road is open to you," one university president told his graduating class several years ago, "except for the one that leads up your parents' driveway." He spoke too soon. Over half of young unmarried adults live with their parents.[6] As urban and suburban rents rise and more and more of America's single-family homes become empty nests, this lifestyle is rapidly regaining popularity.

At the other extreme of the social and economic scale, unmarrieds live lives of poverty. Inner cities have the most concentrated populations of never-marrieds and single parents. These people face all the previously noted burdens, but tend also to be educationally disadvantaged and discriminated against in the workplace. Many are unskilled laborers who have watched their job market evaporate since 1980. They live far away from the most promising job markets and often cannot afford the costs of transportation. Many come from broken families. Others are helping to support parents as well as themselves, or are working their way through school. Crime is an everyday reality and an ever-present threat. For the poorest never-marrieds, life is bleak indeed.

The reality of the never-married lifestyle, then, is far from its carefree image. Thirty-two percent of never-marrieds say they are "stressed out," compared to 26% of marrieds. And nearly half think they are "too busy." Not only do never-marrieds feel more pressures in their lives, they have fewer people to help them get through their day. When asked what relationship is most personally satisfying in their lives, most married people name their spouses, their children, or both. In contrast, over half of all never-marrieds name their best friends. Twenty-one percent list parents and 13% mention their children.[7] Married people, of course, have these people to turn to as well.

Never-marrieds are less established in their communities. They move more often. Their careers are newer and less stable, their professional friends and contacts fewer, their ties to church weaker. Whereas only one in twenty spouses describes himself or herself as lonely, one-fifth of all never-married adults—23% of men and 14% of women—call themselves lonely.

The Good Samaritan Was Married

Marriage and parenthood draw people out of themselves and toward others. Survey after survey points out that these events transform people's priorities from being relatively self-centered and ambitious to being relatively altruistic and

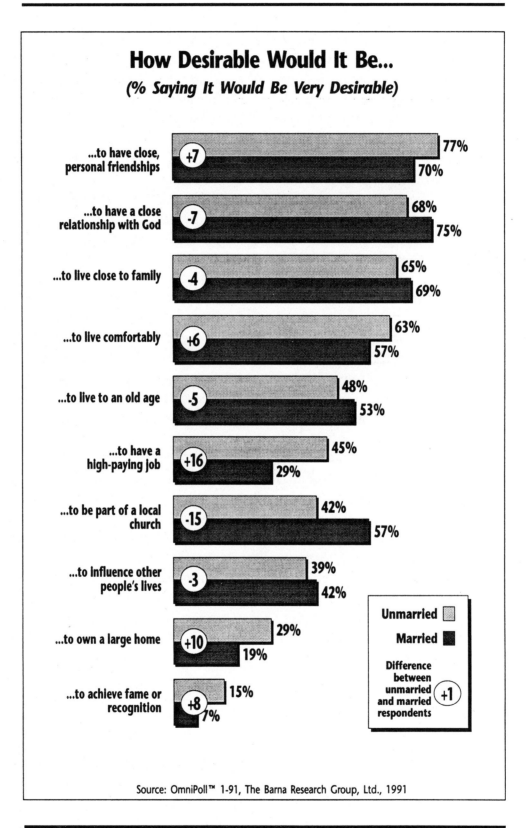

How Desirable Would It Be...
(% Saying It Would Be Very Desirable)

...to have close, personal friendships · +7 · 77% / 70%

...to have a close relationship with God · -7 · 68% / 75%

...to live close to family · -4 · 65% / 69%

...to live comfortably · +6 · 63% / 57%

...to live to an old age · -5 · 48% / 53%

...to have a high-paying job · +16 · 45% / 29%

...to be part of a local church · -15 · 42% / 57%

...to influence other people's lives · -3 · 39% / 42%

...to own a large home · +10 · 29% / 19%

...to achieve fame or recognition · +8 · 15% / 7%

Unmarried ▢
Married ■

Difference between unmarried and married respondents +1

Source: OmniPoll™ 1-91, The Barna Research Group, Ltd., 1991

relational. Unmarrieds, of course, have never made that transition. Compared to married couples, they place a higher value on personal friendships; on having high-paying jobs; on owning a large home; and on becoming famous. At the same time, they place a lower value on a close relationship with God; on being part of a local church; on living close to family; on being able not to have to work for a living; on enjoying good health; and on living to an old age.[8]

Not surprisingly, their philosophies of life differ as well. Nearly half say they live without any particular philosophy at all, compared to only 30% of marrieds. What philosophies never-marrieds have are more secular, more self-centered, more hedonistic and more libertarian than those of other Americans.

One-third of all never-marrieds base their philosophies primarily on nonreligious principles. Only about one-seventh of marrieds do so. Never-marrieds are less likely to believe that people are basically good, that America is a Christian nation, that there is such a thing as absolute truth and that the next day will be better than the one before. On the other hand, they are more likely than marrieds are to believe that one's first responsibility is to oneself, that the purpose of life is enjoyment and personal fulfillment, that one can tell how successful a person is by examining what they own, that everyone has a right to freedom and responsibility, that God helps those who help themselves and that "it is better to get even than to get mad." Never-marrieds are also less concerned than average Americans about violence, sex, profanity and "nontraditional values" on television.[9]

This paints a pretty dismal picture of the hearts of never-married Americans. But it is worth keeping a few facts in mind before judging Never-Married America and finding it wanting. Many of these people are competing in the workforce for the first time, competing for dates and mates, and they have only recently finished competing for grades. Their self-centeredness may well reflect their peculiar—and temporary—station in life. It may also reflect the absence of other people in their lives who directly depend on them. Most never-marrieds get married, and become more altruistic, less materialistic and more spiritually focused in the process. Their attitudes change even more radically when they become parents. And though never-marrieds on average are more likely than marrieds to believe, for instance, in the virtue of vengeance, the numbers are still pretty low: only 19% believe in vengeance, and only 8% believe in it strongly.

They Hate to Wait

The concept of waiting until marriage to become sexually active is nearly dead in America. Sexual activity is commonplace for never-marrieds. Nearly 80% of the never-married adults we surveyed had had a sexual relationship with another never-married adult. Though some groups are more sexually active than others, the numbers are pretty sizeable for a whole range of groups: Men: 84%. Women: 70%. Ages 28-36: 92%. Church attenders: 72%. Frequent Bible readers: 76%. Born-again Christians: 66%.[10]

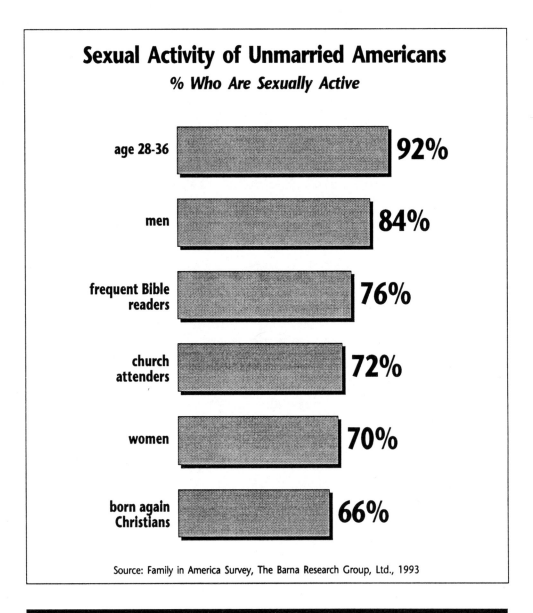

Sexual Activity of Unmarried Americans
% Who Are Sexually Active

age 28-36	92%
men	84%
frequent Bible readers	76%
church attenders	72%
women	70%
born again Christians	66%

Source: Family in America Survey, The Barna Research Group, Ltd., 1993

These numbers do not reflect current sexual activity, only past sexual activity. They tell quite a story nonetheless: many Americans no longer believe sexual activity belongs only within marriage. This is a fundamental change for our society. For instance, in 1965, almost 70% of women under 30 considered premarital sex "always" or "almost always" wrong. But only 22% felt the same way in 1986.[11] This is a true upheaval in one of the most important human and social morals, and it has taken place over the span of only about 20 years.

The destigmatization of premarital sex has ramifications not only for the stability of marriage and families, but also for the rate of divorce, the rate of single parenthood and abortion and the rate of venereal disease. Sexual activity before marriage increases all of these undesirable outcomes.

Will sexual values ever return to the way they were? The sheer human costs of nonmarital sex may eventually reverse the trend. Some future social upheaval may cause sexual values to revert. But sex is getting more and more attention in America, especially within this group, and has been losing its association with marriage and childbearing for some time. It is more likely that improved quality, use and availability of contraception and greater social acceptance will enable sexual activity to remain high for never-marrieds, and for the rest of Unmarried America, for the foreseeable future.

Still Wrong, For Now

One kind of sexual activity that remains off limits for most people, though, is adultery. Despite the trend toward premarital sex, adultery is still considered wrong in America to a far greater extent than it is in post-Christian Europe. (Philosopher Russell Kirk traces adultery's stigma to the lasting influence of Nathaniel Hawthorne's The Scarlet Letter, which was written in Puritan times.)[12]

But it is not surprising to find that as marriage loses its uniqueness in America, adultery is gradually losing its taboo. One-quarter of all never-married adults have had a sexual relationship with a person who was still married to someone else.[13] The highest rates of this kind of sexual activity were among men, among suburban-dwellers and among people with less intense religious beliefs, background and involvement. Infidelity in America may never attain the same level of acceptability it has achieved in Europe, but we are certainly experiencing a trend in that direction.

Unmarried With Children

In the last thirty years, while the fertility rate among American women declined, the rate of childbearing outside marriage skyrocketed. In 1960, one in twenty births was nonmarital—that is, born to an unwed mother. In 1990, the rate was one in four.[14] The newborn infants at a local hospital's maternity ward wear plastic bracelets with their vital information: time of birth, weight, sex, first name and last name. The last name of the mother, that is. Why does a baby not wear its father's name on its bracelet? Because it is more likely than ever that the baby was born to an unmarried mother. Welcome to another fast-growing part of Unmarried America: Unmarried America with Children.

The numbers are sobering. In 1970, 13%, or about one in eight, families in America were one-parent families. By 1990, the figure had grown to 21%—more than one in five.[15] *Almost one-quarter of the births in 1985 were to unmarried women,*[16] compared to only one-tenth of the births between 1960 and 1968. In 1990, nearly 10 million women lived with children under 21 whose fathers were absent. Of those, 2.5 million had been divorced and were now remarried. Three million were currently divorced and 1.3 million were separated from their husbands. Almost 3 million—30%—had never married in the first place.[17] Today one in twelve children lives with one parent who has never married.[18]

Much, but by no means all, of single parenthood follows racial lines. White adults are slightly less likely than the population as a whole to be single parents. Hispanic adults, on the other hand, are more likely: one-third of hispanic families are single-parent families. And black families are *predominantly* single: over 50% of black households have only one parent.[19]

Single parenthood is usually single motherhood. Thirteen percent of white American families are maintained only by mothers; four percent are maintained only by fathers. Contrast this with hispanic families: 24% are maintained only by mothers, and seven percent are maintained only by fathers. In black America, the numbers are astounding. Mothers head 46% of black families. Fathers, head an additional six percent. That means that fewer than one out of every seven black single parents is a father. Concern over the missing "father figure" is well-founded: fathers are present in *barely more than half* of all black families.[20]

The economics of single-parent families are disturbing. Fewer single parents have full-time jobs than do unmarried nonparents. Over 80% of women raising children themselves cannot afford modestly priced houses in the area where they live, compared to only 30% of married couple families.[21] Though only 9% of white two-parent families live below the official poverty level, 44% of white one-

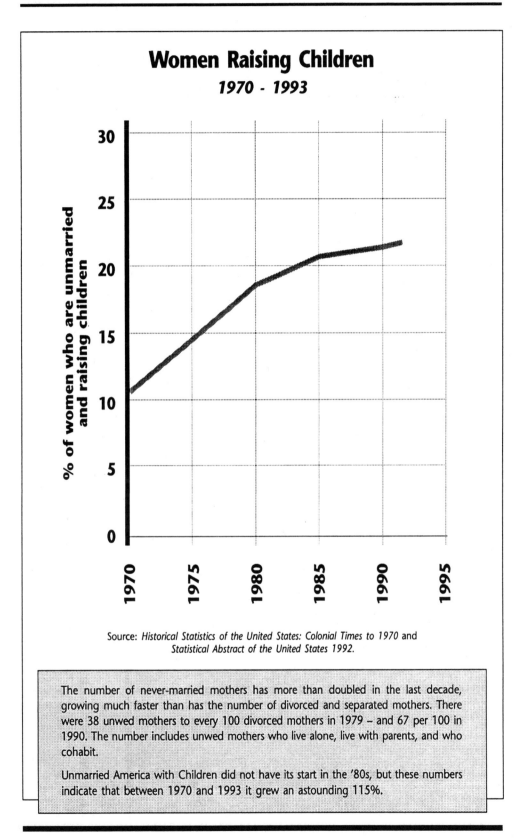

Women Raising Children
1970 - 1993

Source: *Historical Statistics of the United States: Colonial Times to 1970* and
Statistical Abstract of the United States 1992.

The number of never-married mothers has more than doubled in the last decade, growing much faster than has the number of divorced and separated mothers. There were 38 unwed mothers to every 100 divorced mothers in 1979 – and 67 per 100 in 1990. The number includes unwed mothers who live alone, live with parents, and who cohabit.

Unmarried America with Children did not have its start in the '80s, but these numbers indicate that between 1970 and 1993 it grew an astounding 115%.

parent families do. Twenty percent of black two-parent families are defined as poor; 67% of black one-parent families are. Thirty percent of hispanic two-parent families are below the line, as opposed to 68% of hispanic one-parent families.[22] Only about one-quarter of all single mothers and three-quarters of all divorced or separated mothers are awarded child-support. Even then, only about half of these women actually receive what is legally due them. The average amount a mother received in 1989 was under $3,000.[23] Murphy Brown or no Murphy Brown, single parenthood in America is far from a glamorous or comfortable lifestyle.

Life in the Single-Parent Lane

The experiences of single parents produce lifestyles and attitudes that are more home-centered and introverted, more like married couples than unmarried singles. Single parents are less likely than unmarrieds as a whole to describe themselves as lonely, and much more likely to say they feel "stressed out."

Single parents are less likely to wish they had more close friends. They tend to look for new friends at school, rather than at work, community organizations or exercise clubs. Americans generally prefer small churches to large ones, but single parents prefer them even more. They are less likely to read or exercise for recreation, or to volunteer their free time to help non-church organizations.

When asked whether they spend more or less of their time on activities like working at their jobs, being with their families, watching television, going to church, visiting friends and so on, never-marrieds without children were much more likely to respond that they spend the same amount of time doing these things as they did last year. The calendars of never-marrieds with children, on the other hand, reflect constant change in how they allocate their time. Last year's behavioral patterns are not necessarily good predictions of this year's schedule. Unmarried parenthood, then, puts people's lives in a greater state of flux.[24]

Perhaps because they find them less attainable, single parents value family, free time, money, comfort and their careers more than is the case among unmarrieds without children. All involve time and money, two commodities unmarried parents are usually short of, and the 1990-1991 recession hit these people hard. Single parents were significantly likely to say they were tightening their belts during the recession. When asked how they would adjust their spending patterns, many more single parents than married adults told us they were cutting back on entertainment (71%), eating out less (70%), reducing their driving (49%) and moving to cheaper housing (24%). Married and remarried people, who have much

Single Parents' Changing Priorities

How They Spent Their Time, Compared to the Previous Year

	Single Parent	Married Parent
Church or religious activities	47% / 36% / 16%	27% / 47% / 24%
Watching T.V.	42% / 36% / 22%	40% / 43% / 16%
Volunteering their time	34% / 36% / 29%	29% / 50% / 20%
Reading for pleasure	40% / 25% / 35%	27% / 39% / 34%
With their friends	41% / 22% / 37%	31% / 47% / 21%
Exercising or working out	35% / 25% / 40%	31% / 41% / 27%
At home with their family	29% / 26% / 45%	5% / 44% / 50%
Seeking additional formal education	27% / 22% / 48%	37% / 38% / 21%
Working at their job	16% / 29% / 56%	17% / 30% / 38%

Are You Spending...

■ Less Time
□ Same Amount of Time
■ More Time

...compared to one year ago?

Source: OmniPoll™ 1-91, The Barna Research Group, Ltd., 1991

higher incomes, were much less likely to say they were changing their behavior. Even divorced people and widows were less sensitive to the weak economy than unmarried parents.

Single parents are optimistic about the future. This is partly an outgrowth of the fact that they have more faith than others do in institutions like schools, churches, hospitals, government, the media and nonprofit organizations. They value involvement in those institutions, even though they are less involved themselves. Optimism is also partly attributable to their sense of self-reliance and ability to survive. Most single parents feel that people need to be responsible for their own actions, that "God helps those who help themselves." Single parents are also more likely than other unmarrieds to feel that one reaps what one sows, and that most people are poor because they are lazy. These attitudes may result from grappling with all the challenges single parents face and overcome in their daily lives, without even the help of a spouse.[25]

Unmarrieds with children are in between worlds. In some ways, their lifestyles and thoughts are distinctively single. In many others they are more like marrieds. Single parents' experiences leave their mark, which is manifests itself through a greater zeal for the "good life" and a greater respect for personal responsibility and initiative in spite of all the barriers unmarried parents face in their daily lives.

N   O   T   E   S

1   *Historical Statistics of the United States: Colonial Times to 1970*, p. 19 and *Statistical Abstract of the United States 1992*, p. 91.

2   *Statistical Abstract of the United States 1992*, p. 44.

3   Barna Research Group, Ltd., Family in America survey (Glendale, California: Barna Research Group, Ltd., 1992).

4   Barna Research Group, Ltd., OmniPoll™ 2-91 (Glendale, California: Barna Research Group, Ltd., 1991).

5   Barna Research Group, Ltd., OmniPoll™ 1-91 (Glendale, California: Barna Research Group, Ltd., 1991).

6   *Statistical Abstract*, p. 52.

7   Family in America survey.

8   Barna Research Group, Ltd., OmniPoll™ 1-91 (Glendale, California: Barna Research Group, Ltd., 1991).

9   Barna Research Group, Ltd., Family Support and Views survey (Glendale, California: Barna Research Group, Ltd., 1992).

10 Barna Research Group, Ltd., Family in America survey.

11 Popenoe, David, "Flight from the Nuclear Family: Trends of the Past Three Decades," *Public Perspective* (March-April 1991). p. 19.

12 Kirk, Russell, *The Conservative Mind* (Lake Bluff, Ill: Regnery Books, 1986).

13 Barna Research Group, Ltd., Family in America survey.

14 Popenoe, p. 19.

15 *Statistical Abstract,* p. 46.

16 Bumpass, Larry and James Sweet, *Children's Experience in Single-Parent Families: Implications of Cohabitation and Marital Transitions,* National Survey of Families and Households Working Paper No. 3 (Madison, Wisconsin: Center for Demography and Ecology, University of Wisconsin, June 1989), p. 3.

17 U.S. Bureau of the Census, *Child Support and Alimony: 1989* (Washington, DC: U.S. Government Printing Office, 1989).

18 *Statistical Abstract,* p. 55.

19 *Statistical Abstract,* p. 47-48.

20 Ibid.

21 U.S. Bureau of the Census, *Who Can Afford to Buy a House?* (Washington, DC: U.S. Government Printing Office, May 1991).

22 *Statistical Abstract,* p. 457.

23 *Child Support and Alimony: 1989,* p. 1.

24 Barna Research Group, Ltd., OmniPoll™ 1-91.

25 Barna Research Group, Ltd., OmniPoll™ 1-91.

C H A P T E R   F O U R

Marriage And Its Alternatives

*T*he trends may make it sound as if unmarried Americans are against the very idea of marriage. They are not. Nine in ten Americans will eventually marry. Thirty-eight percent of never-marrieds "definitely want to" marry, and 46% more "would like to." Nine percent are cool to the idea, and only 5% "definitely do not want to get married." [1]

Those that want to marry find companionship, love, children, commitment and family the top attractions. But the appeal of companionship dwarfs the other benefits in importance, perhaps because of the loneliness many never-marrieds feel. Six in ten hopeful never-marrieds listed companionship as one of the most appealing reasons to walk down the aisle.[2]

But What Is a Family?

When many never-marrieds speak of marriage and family, they have traditional images in their minds. But a sizable number do not. Just as many unmarrieds are redefining the meaning of the never-married lifestyle, many are redefining the American family.

Only one-third of unmarrieds think adults need to be legally married to have stable families. Though unmarrieds tend to conceive of marriage as a permanent arrangement between two people, and tend to think that America would be better off under stricter divorce laws, they are more likely than others to consider cohabiters without children, cohabiters with children and homosexual cohabiters to be "families." Never-married women are even more accepting of these alternative definitions than are never-married men.[3]

Though they remain enthusiastic about marriage, unmarrieds are still four times more likely than married adults to feel that it is better to go through life unmarried than to get married. Never-marrieds are far more likely than the average adult to prefer today's family values, or a new values system altogether, to the values of the '50s.[4]

Raising Children Differently

Never-marrieds' attitudes about childrearing are decidedly untraditional. It could be because of their youth, or their culture, or their own pasts, or just their unfamiliarity with marriage. For whatever reason, unmarrieds downplay the importance of marriage, of tradition and even of parents themselves in the lives of children. To these people, "parental control" sounds like an oxymoron.

One reason unmarrieds are less concerned about parental influence on their children is that they think parents have little sway in the first place. Almost all never-marrieds consider teaching values to children a parent's responsibility. But only 19% of them think parents are actually the most influential force in teaching values to children, as opposed to 33% of marrieds. They give schools and their children's friends a greater share of that responsibility, and churches a smaller share. Ninety percent of marrieds think children are very likely to have successful upbringings if they are raised by happily married, natural parents—but only 82% of never-marrieds agree. And never-marrieds are less sanguine about the possibility that a child adopted by a happily married couple will be raised successfully.[5] On the other hand, only 27% consider it unfair for cohabiting, unmarried parents to raise children, compared to 46% of husbands and wives.

In the high-profile brouhaha between Dan Quayle and the writers of the highly rated television program Murphy Brown, never-marrieds tended to side with the screenwriters. Almost all never-marrieds (92%) personally know at least one single parent. Yet they do not consider single parenthood as difficult a lifestyle as divorced or even married people do. Half of them—about the same rate as marrieds—think a single-parent family is fundamentally no different from a two-parent family. What about having to enroll the children in day care? No problem. Unmarrieds feel better than husbands and wives do about the effect of full-time day care on children. They are also more comfortable with families where both

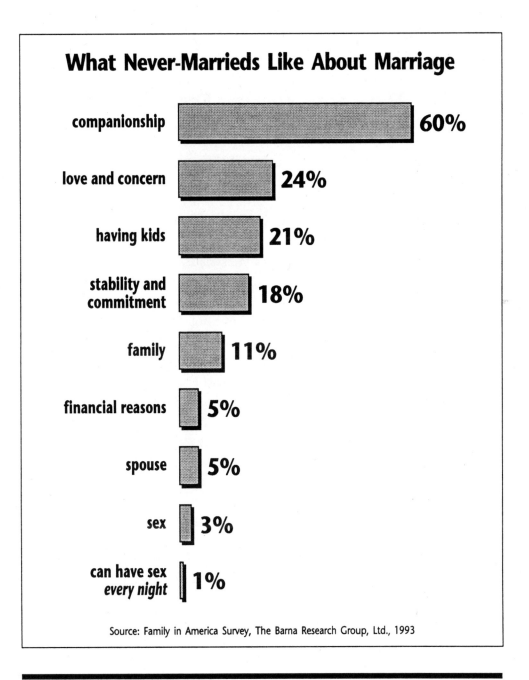

What Never-Marrieds Like About Marriage

companionship	60%
love and concern	24%
having kids	21%
stability and commitment	18%
family	11%
financial reasons	5%
spouse	5%
sex	3%
can have sex every night	1%

Source: Family in America Survey, The Barna Research Group, Ltd., 1993

parents work. Twenty-two percent of never-marrieds think a family is more likely to be happy when both parents work. Only 15% of marrieds feel the same way.

These (less and less) unconventional attitudes show up in another visible area: the issue of sex education in schools. Here acceptance of premarital sex combines with low appraisals of the influence of parents on their children. The result: Over 70% of never-marrieds think public schools should encourage people to use condoms, compared to 38% of marrieds and divorced people and only 24% of widows. Only 20% of never-marrieds want schools to discourage premarital sex.[6]

The Trend Toward Cohabitation

The widespread practice of living together before marriage (cohabiting) burst on the scene less than thirty years ago. Since then, more and more never-marrieds have been finding it appealing. Today 60% of never-marrieds think it wise to live with one's partner before getting married.[7] One-quarter of all Americans have cohabiting experience, as have half of all people who were recently married. The trend toward living together outside marriage may be new, but it is powerful.

It should not be surprising that cohabiters share untraditional views of marriage and human commitment. But marriage is still the ultimate goal for most cohabitants. In their eyes, cohabitation is more of an economic than philosophical arrangement. For instance, people who have not completed high school usually plan to marry their roommates. Blacks are more likely to plan to marry than whites are. But some cohabiters are less traditional: college graduates are more likely to view the arrangement as an alternative to marriage than as a step toward it.[8] Even so, most cohabiting college graduates eventually take the plunge and get married.

Cohabiting relationships have other nuances as well. Short-term relationships are usually preludes to marriage, while long-term relationships serve as alternatives to marriage. People who have lived together for three or more years are less likely to plan to marry. So are people over 25 years old.[9] Never-marrieds tend to view cohabitation as a prelude to marriage, while divorced people are less likely to marry their live-in partners.

To people who cohabit, their intentions largely determine whether or not they feel such an arrangement is morally right. Every subculture sees the family differently, so it only makes sense that prior marital status, education, income, race and age—to name a few—all color people's appraisal of cohabitation as an acceptable lifestyle. For instance, almost six in ten young unmarried people

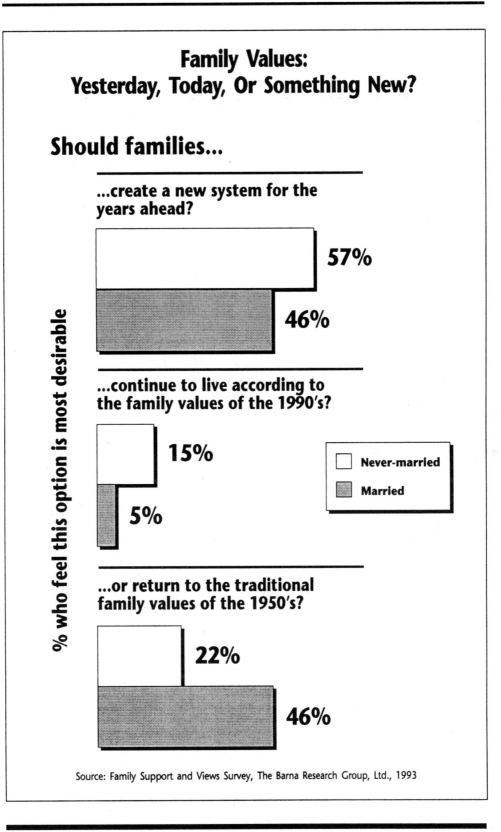

**Family Values:
Yesterday, Today, Or Something New?**

Should families...

...create a new system for the
years ahead?

57%

46%

...continue to live according to
the family values of the 1990's?

15%

5%

Never-married

Married

...or return to the traditional
family values of the 1950's?

22%

46%

% who feel this option is most desirable

Source: Family Support and Views Survey, The Barna Research Group, Ltd., 1993

believe cohabitation is acceptable if the couple intends to marry. About half believe it is acceptable if the couple is testing their relationship for permanent compatibility. But only about three in ten consider it acceptable if the couple has no interest in marriage.[10] At the same time, these young unmarrieds apply their moral values only to themselves and tend not to judge others—even those immersed in equivalent lifestyles and experiences.

Don't Commit, Cohabit

Finally, cohabiters share less commitment to marriage than do married couples. People with experience cohabiting are less likely to believe that marriage is a lifetime experience. They are more likely to approve of divorce for an unhappily married couple with a young child; more likely to think a spouse should overlook occasional adultery on the part of their spouse; more likely to approve of premarital sex for adults; and more likely to approve of unmarried women having children without getting married.[11]

Tragically, these attitudes may be manifesting themselves in a comparatively high divorce rate. People who had lived with others besides their spouse are 84% more likely to divorce than people who did not cohabit. Even people who lived only with their spouse before marrying are nearly 50% more likely to divorce than people who did not cohabit at all.[12]

Even though marriage is usually the ultimate goal of cohabiters, the marriages most are anticipating are unusually fragile. People who live together are more likely to envision their marriages ending in divorce than people who do not. They suspect the institution of marriage, they value individualism and they avoid commitments even more than other never-marrieds do. Cohabiters who marry are inclined to take family responsibilities more lightly. They worry less about occasional sexual unfaithfulness, premarital sex, single parenthood, full-time working mothers and of divorce than unmarrieds who do not live together, let alone other Americans.[13] And they divorce much more often. Studies have associated cohabitation with greater marital conflict and with poor communication between mates.[14]

If unmarrieds as a group are untraditional in their family values, cohabiters are even more so. Notwithstanding the popular image of people who live together, nearly one-third of cohabiting households include children.[15] Not surprisingly, cohabiters view child-rearing differently than do married people. More cohabiters than non-cohabiters approve of mothers with preschoolers working full-time and of children under three years old being cared for all day in child care centers. One-

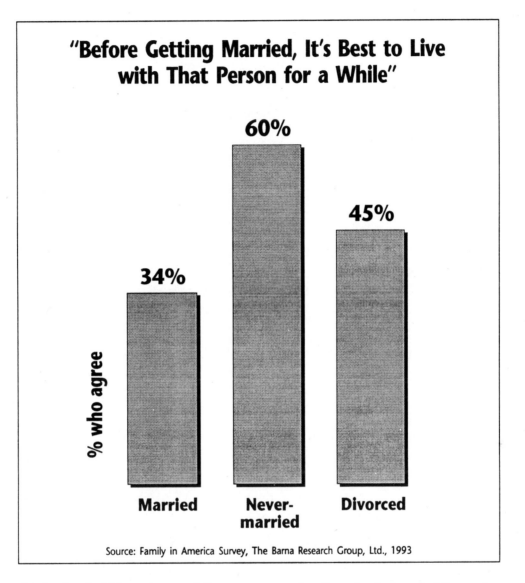

"Before Getting Married, It's Best to Live with That Person for a While"

60%

45%

34%

% who agree

Married **Never-married** **Divorced**

Source: Family in America Survey, The Barna Research Group, Ltd., 1993

third of cohabiting parents fail to marry each other. In fact, cohabiters who become parents are only slightly more likely to marry afterwards than they would have been before parenthood.[16]

Cohabiters, then, send mixed signals on their attitudes and lifestyles. Few explicitly reject the idea of marriage. In all, about three-fifths of all first-time cohabiting relationships end in marriage rather than breaking up.[17] Yet for all their verbal affirmations of marriage, cohabiters are decidedly less committed to the institution. Many profess respect for marriage by living together as a way of preventing divorce—yet cohabiters are more likely to be divorced. Many defend cohabitation as a way of protecting children from having to live in an unstable home; yet they produce and raise children outside a married family environment.

The Complex Morality of Cohabitation

Despite its surge in popularity, cohabitation is still somewhat controversial. What kind of people approve of living together? Adults younger than 35 are much more accepting of the practice than their elders. They grew up after 1970, when the rate of cohabitation began to rise steeply. Most cohabiters actually belong to this generation. As they age, the next group—people 25 and younger—are even more accepting of cohabitation. Members of Jewish, Episcopalian, Catholic and Presbyterian denominations are actually above average in their approval. People in the northeast and in the west and residents of the core areas of large cities are also more approving than average. And ethnic minorities are more approving than whites—but only if the couple living together intend to marry. Otherwise, they are actually less approving than whites.

Despite the complex moral issues surrounding cohabitation, some researchers see a general trend in the rise of cohabitation. They interpret the high rate of breaking up among people who live together and the high rate of divorce among the ones who marry to mean that cohabitation is becoming a new stage of courtship.[18]

Not Looking Back

Various studies show that marriages preceded by cohabitation are more likely to end in divorce. Others show the prevalence of poverty in single-parent families. Another has shown that children of single-parent and step-families are two to three times more likely to have developmental, learning and emotional problems.[19] It is estimated that three out of four children of cohabiting couples will spend some part of their childhood in a single-parent family because of the high rate of divorce among formerly cohabiting spouses, and because of the high number of cohabiters who remain unmarried while raising children.[20]

How do unmarrieds respond to findings like these? Will they return to more traditional values?

So far, the answer is no. Never-marrieds tend to prefer the world as it is today. And fewer of them expect the pendulum to swing back. Will America return to the "good old days" of the '50s? Never-marrieds think not, by nearly a 4-to-1 margin. Will most people who get married be divorced within five years? More than half of all never-marrieds think so, a greater proportion than any other group—including divorced people. Will marriage be replaced by cohabitation in the next few years? Over half of all unmarrieds believe it will. For Unmarried America, the new order is here to stay.[21]

N   O   T   E   S

1   Barna Research Group, Ltd., Family in America survey (Glendale, California: Barna Research Group, Ltd., 1992).

2   Ibid.

3   Ibid.

4   Barna Research Group, Ltd., Family Support and Views survey (Glendale, California: Barna Research Group, Ltd.,1992).

5   Family in America survey.

6   Family Support and Views survey.

7   Family in America survey.

8   Bumpass, Larry and James Sweet, *Young Adults' Views of Marriage, Cohabitation, and Family*, National Survey of Families and Households Working Paper No. 33 (Madison, Wisconsin: Center for Demography and Ecology, University of Wisconsin), p. 4.

9   Ibid., pp. 8-9.

10 Ibid., p. 12.

11 Ibid., p.20.

12 Ibid., p. 16.

13 Ibid., pp. 19-20.

14 Thomson, Elizabeth and Ugo Colella, *Cohabitation and Marital Stability: Quality or Commitment?* National Survey of Families and Households Working Paper No. 23 (Madison, Wisconsin: Center for Demography and Ecology, University of Wisconsin, June 1989), p. 9.

15 *Statistical Abstract of the United States 1992*, p. 45.

16 Bumpass, Larry L. and James Sweet, *Children's Experience in Single-Parent Families: Implications of Cohabitation and Marital Transitions,* [National Survey of Families and Households Working Paper No. 3] (Madison, Wisconsin: Center for Demography and Ecology, University of Wisconsin, April, 1989), p. 7.

17 *Young Adults' Views of Marriage, Cohabitation, and Family*, p. 1.

18 *Cohabitation and Marital Stability: Quality or Commitment?* p. 1.

19 Popenoe, David, "Flight from the Nuclear Family: Trends of the Past Three Decades," *Public Perspective* (March-April 1991). p. 20.

20   *Children's Experience in Single-Parent Families: Implications of Cohabitation and Marital Transitions*, p. 7.

21   Barna Research Group, Ltd., Family in America survey.

C H A P T E R   F I V E

Family Affair: How Singles See the Church

Young never-marrieds are perhaps the least churched of Americans. Slightly more than one in four never-marrieds, and one in seven unchurched never-marrieds, has religious beliefs that classify him as a born-again Christian. (Nearly 40% of marrieds do.) Unmarrieds tend to see the church as irrelevant, unfamiliar and unfriendly. A survey of ours showed that only 43% had attended a church worship service in the previous month, compared to 60% of marrieds and widows and 57% of divorced adults. Among never-married men, the figure was just 38%.[1]

When they are attending church, never-marrieds are less involved. We found that only 22% of them had attended a Sunday school class, compared to one-third of marrieds. Only 13% had attended a small group, compared to one-fifth of marrieds. Never-marrieds also had read the Bible less often than marrieds (33% compared to 44% within the past week).[2]

Alongside this detachment, however, lie generally favorable impressions of Christianity. Over half of all unchurched never-marrieds say religion is important in their everyday lives, and 70% have a favorable impression of Christianity. Nearly three-quarters of all unchurched never-marrieds went to church regularly sometime in the past, and more than half still have favorable attitudes about their local Christian churches.[3]

So unmarrieds' apathy is, in a way, surprising. What is keeping them out of church? Singles are likely to point to busy schedules, lack of interest, non-Christian beliefs, negative experiences and negative opinions as reasons not to get involved. Many even say they do not know.[4]

These are the surface reasons. But the real reason is relevance. If unmarrieds found attending and serving in a church a compelling experience, they would be interested and make room in their schedules. They do not. Only 4% consider the church "very sensitive" towards the needs of never-married adults. While our research suggests that there is no deep animosity among any unmarrieds toward the Christian church,[5] unchurched never-marrieds are far from convinced that the pastors and people of America's churches care about them, or that they have much to offer. Consequently, only 15% of them expect to attend church in the next six months.[6]

Never-marrieds tend to be suspicious of organized religion, but not terribly so. For instance, 56% of them felt favorably toward the Baptist Church, 55% toward the Catholic Church, 46% toward the Methodist Church, 39% toward the Lutheran Church and 38% toward the Presbyterian Church. On the other hand, very few never-marrieds think "very favorably" toward these churches: only 21%, 23%, 12%, 14% and 7%, respectively.

If never-marrieds do not feel favorably disposed toward these churches, they are inclined not to have an opinion rather than to express a negative one. Half of all respondents replied "don't know" about Presbyterians, 49% about Lutherans, 38% about Methodists, 27% about Baptists and 18% about Roman Catholics. Note that these are in just about the opposite order as the positive impressions. These impressions are tied to never-marrieds' ignorance of these groups and the irrelevance they perceive. So there is plenty of opportunity for churches to make an impression on today's generation of Americans. And there is even more opportunity to reach never-marrieds, since they are the group most likely not to have an opinion.[7]

Small Is Beautiful

Unchurched never-marrieds prefer small churches, especially churches with fewer than 100 people. They like their services on Sunday morning. They prefer informal services to formal services. They value congregational participation. They prefer contemporary music to traditional hymns, but like a mix of the two even more. They prefer some tradition to either a lot or none at all. They are more open to churches with women pastors; however, only 10% would prefer a female pastor, compared to only 4% of all adults. They prefer churches with no denominational affiliation (here their distrust of organized religion shows) and churches that are involved in their communities, particularly those that help the needy.[8]

Whereas unchurched marrieds say they would prefer their initial introduction to a church to be through a Sunday service, never-marrieds feel completely differently. They do not want to become involved in churches through either services or Bible classes. For them, the way into church is not the front door. Instead, over half say they are interested in getting involved in groups that meet socially. Even more are interested in volunteer efforts to help the needy in their communities. Never-marrieds also find concerts, seminars or other special events that a church might hold to be more alluring than a simple visit on Sunday morning.

These preferences make unchurched never-marrieds a challenging group for churches to reach. They require creative and innovative approaches, not retrofitted traditional ones. But what might be the greatest challenge of all is hinted at by one attitude these people share: they are less likely to be attracted to churches that emphasize Bible study and teaching. That is quite an obstacle to overcome for churches that want their members' faith to be more than skin deep.

Before you throw your hands up in despair, though, recognize the context for such a perspective. Single adults are not so much adamantly opposed to Bible-based teaching as they are expecting that such instruction will be unkind in its response to the single lifestyle and irrelevant to what singles are searching for in life.

Tips for Seeker-Hostile Churches

What is the best way for a church to advertise in order to influence this religion-resistant part of America? The need for innovative approaches is best illustrated by not an example, but a counterexample. A commercial for the local Yellow Pages directory lampoons retailers who do not advertise, as being people who go to great lengths to avoid selling their products at any cost. Imagine what the phone company would do with a church that wanted to alienate and discourage never-marrieds who visit:

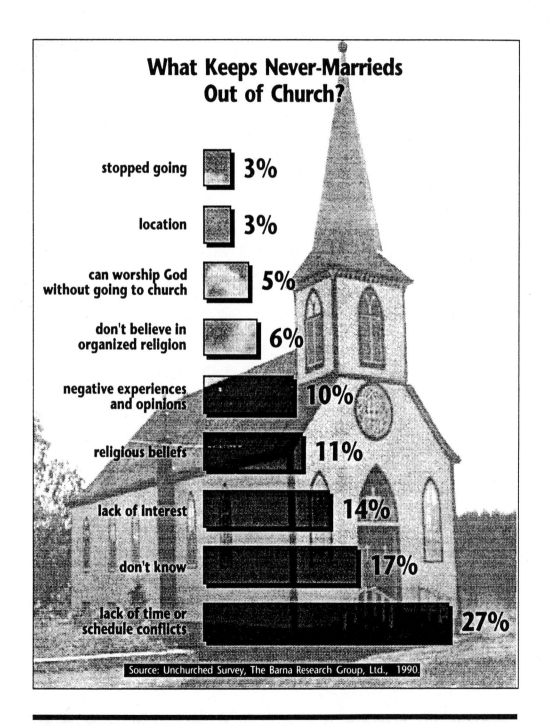

What Keeps Never-Marrieds Out of Church?

- stopped going — 3%
- location — 3%
- can worship God without going to church — 5%
- don't believe in organized religion — 6%
- negative experiences and opinions — 10%
- religious beliefs — 11%
- lack of interest — 14%
- don't know — 17%
- lack of time or schedule conflicts — 27%

Source: Unchurched Survey, The Barna Research Group, Ltd., 1990.

"First, we send the senior pastor to their homes after they visit. They hate that. Just the pastoral visit turns off more than half of them! Then, if they keep coming, we do some telemarketing. And we're filming a commercial next week, because we found out that TV advertising bothers them *even more!"*

Unchurched never-marrieds *are* interested in information about churches they might visit. But it is important to give them information they care about, in a way that will not offend them. Singles consider a church's location, denomination, doctrine, history and service times important to know. Fewer, but still more than half, want to know a church's size. They are even less interested in the title of a given week's sermon, the availability of child care (with the powerful exception of single parents) or the pastor's name.[9]

Churches courting never-marrieds would be wise to avoid a few church followup techniques to which this group is opposed. Never-marrieds typically disdain home visits by a pastor or another church member even more than other people groups do. They especially dislike wearing nametags when visiting a church.[10]

As always, the best advertising is word-of-mouth. Seventy-eight percent of unchurched never-marrieds say an invitation from a friend might persuade them to come along to church. This explains why "lifestyle evangelism" is replacing home visitation and in-the-spotlight identification of church visitors as a common way of helping churches grow.[11]

A word about direct mail: many people probably overestimate the hostility felt towards unsolicited letters. Cleverly-designed pieces can be turn-ons rather than turn-offs. But at the same time direct mail brings some visitors, it offends others— perhaps more than the numbers it attracts. The new people in the pews on a given Sunday are not the only ones whom a mailing has "reached."

Christianity: Only for Families?

We have already pointed out several findings that suggest that Christianity is of some importance to unchurched never-marrieds, in spite of their apathy toward church. Almost two-thirds of them have some respect for biblically-based philosophy. And 40% say they have made a personal commitment to Jesus Christ that remains important in their lives.

Yet fewer and fewer never-marrieds are churched, and the distance shows. Thirty-seven percent of unchurched adults think people go to heaven because they have confessed their sins and accepted Christ. One-quarter of unchurched never-marrieds feel the same way. More than 40% of unchurched never-marrieds do not know what will happen when they die, compared to only 30% of unchurched adults.[12] Unchurched never-marrieds are less familiar and less involved with Christianity than are other unchurched Americans. Though most of them toy with personal philosophies and think about God, they do not find Christianity particularly compelling nor particularly relevant to their everyday lives.

Why are so many people with spiritual concerns staying away from the church? One reason is that young people, and especially young never-marrieds, increasingly distinguish more and more between formal institutions and what those institutions represent. Unchurched never-marrieds distinguish between theology and organized religion.

Another major reason is not philosophical, so much as cultural. Many never-marrieds stay away from churches because they consider church to be a family affair. Forty-five percent of never-marrieds think the Bible contains a lot of practical advice on marriage and family issues, but only one-third think it has a lot of it for the lives of unmarried adults. They do not see it as a faith for all people, regardless of marital or social status. Instead, most never-marrieds see the Bible as a "family" book and Christianity a "family" religion—and even then, not a tremendously helpful one. A lot of the time, churches do little to change these impressions. Several anecdotes illustrate how Christianity's cultural trappings can become confused with its message:

At one church's marriage preparation seminar a young man raised his hand and asked: "What do you think about what Paul said in First Corinthians? Is it really better not to be married at all?" The teacher was flabbergasted. After an uncomfortable silence she found the words to reassure him that Paul was talking only to Corinthians, not to everyone, and certainly not to this particular class. There was little room in this church's theology for the gift of celibacy.

A megachurch's singles pastor told—actually, pleaded to—his class that the Christian life can be as full before, after, or outside marriage as within it. As he explained that singleness could even be a gift from God, his audience remained unmoved. Their faces reflected not liberation, but longing and skepticism. The singles pastor was telling them one thing, the church's culture quite another.

Many churches make it obvious, sometimes despite their best intentions, that their church culture centers around families, not individuals. They expect unchurched never-marrieds to visit Sunday morning services—which unchurched never-marrieds prefer not to visit cold. Unmarrieds that do visit are directed to the "singles" class, where they will presumably meet their future mates and get with the program. Two-thirds of the people who lead these ministries to unmarried adults, of course, are married.[13]

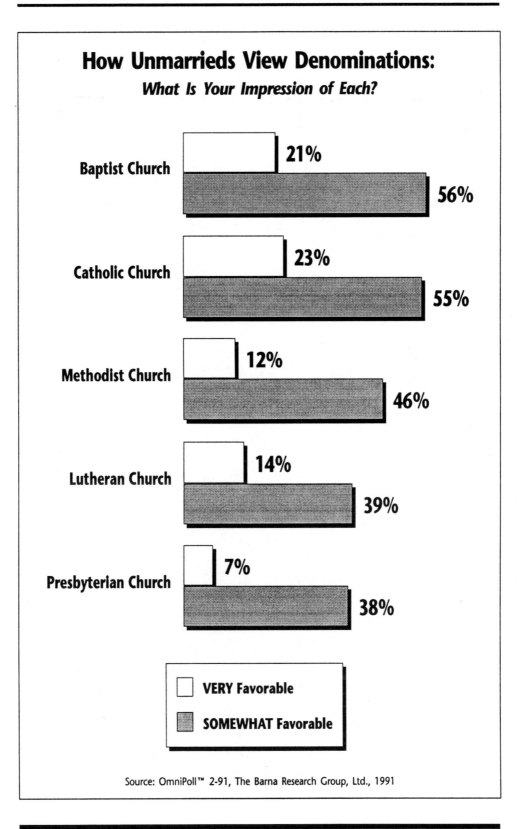

How Unmarrieds View Denominations:
What Is Your Impression of Each?

Baptist Church 21% 56%

Catholic Church 23% 55%

Methodist Church 12% 46%

Lutheran Church 14% 39%

Presbyterian Church 7% 38%

☐ VERY Favorable

▨ SOMEWHAT Favorable

Source: OmniPoll™ 2-91, The Barna Research Group, Ltd., 1991

The Clock is Ticking

The fastest-growing demographic groups in America are *not* traditional families. Every day, traditional families are losing their monopoly on social acceptability. Never-marrieds and other Unmarried Americans prove by their lifestyles, values

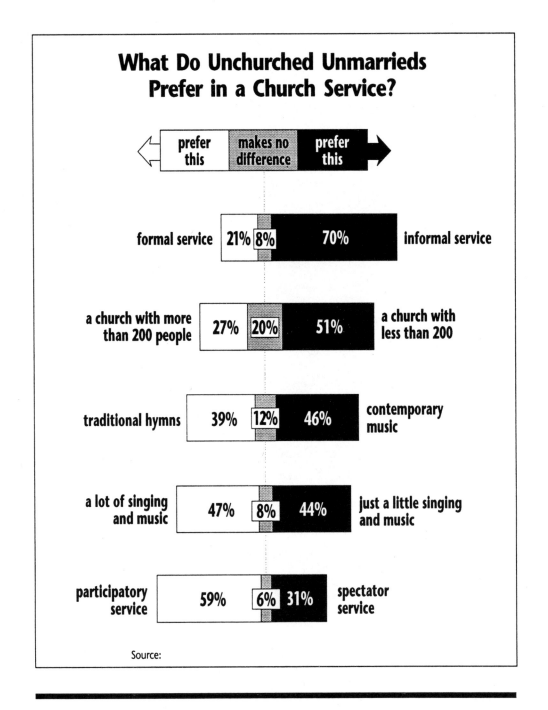

What Do Unchurched Unmarrieds Prefer in a Church Service?

	prefer this	makes no difference	prefer this

formal service	21%	8%	70%	informal service
a church with more than 200 people	27%	20%	51%	a church with less than 200
traditional hymns	39%	12%	46%	contemporary music
a lot of singing and music	47%	8%	44%	just a little singing and music
participatory service	59%	6%	31%	spectator service

Source:

and attitudes that even those who plan to marry expect to have neither traditional marriages nor traditional families.

Surveys repeatedly show that people become more concerned about God and involved with the church after they get married and have children. For a variety of reasons, religion usually plays a greater role within families than outside them. It seems almost inevitable that churches will be most culturally attuned to the needs and wants of families. But rather than trying their hardest to overcome these obstacles to reaching and serving never-marrieds, many churches instead reinforce and even promote the stereotype that only minivans belong in their parking lots. The "family church" is at a great disadvantage in reaching out to non-families. What will become of the church in America if the fastest-growing sectors of the population consider it irrelevant?

Churches are not fated to be insensitive to the needs of unmarrieds. They can be truly effective in reaching never-married Americans if they make an ongoing, thorough commitment to examine their image and ministries to see how they might be made friendlier to unmarrieds. Becoming and staying relevant takes a lot of effort—but it is worth the trouble.

N O T E S

1 Barna Research Group, Ltd., Family in America survey.

2 Ibid.

3 Barna Research Group, Ltd., Unchurched survey (Glendale, California: Barna Research Group, Ltd., 1990).

4 Barna Research Group, Ltd., Unchurched survey.

5 Barna Research Group, Ltd., OmniPoll™ 2-91 survey.

6 Barna Research Group, Ltd., Unchurched survey.

7 Barna Research Group, Ltd., OmniPoll™ 2-91.

8 Barna Research Group, Ltd., Unchurched survey.

9 Barna Research Group, Ltd., Unchurched survey.

10 Ibid.

11 Ibid.

12 Various Barna Research Group surveys, 1990-1992.

13 Jones, Jerry D., ed. *National Single Adult Ministries Resource Directory 1989* (Colorado Springs, CO: Single Adult Ministries Journal, 1989), p.11.

C H A P T E R S I X

The Divorce Revolution and Its Casualties

*T*he familiar chart of American marital status over the last century (see chapter 1 chart, page 8) illustrates the rise of a now-common way of life for Americans: divorce. Today, more than 16 million American adults are currently divorced.[1]

One observer calls the explosion in divorce over the last thirty years a "divorce revolution."[2] But the divorce rate has grown for at least a century (see chapter 1 chart, page 8). It picked up pace and perhaps reached critical mass during the 1970's with the passage of no-fault divorce laws in California in 1970 and other states afterward. Since 1980 the trend has been leveling off.[3] At any rate, at some point along this curve, Americans realized that divorce had become a ubiquitous feature of our country's family life. It will be a powerful force in our lives for the foreseeable future. There is no turning back.

As we will see, divorced adults are a group with not only great diversity, but also with great similarities—similarities coming principally from their experience of living through the destruction of their families. Their attitudes and lifestyles betray the fact that they are never completely "single" in the way that never-marrieds are. They are a subgroup all their own, a permanent and distinct part of Unmarried America.

The Demographics of Divorce

Financially, divorced people are better off than never-marrieds.[4] But their incomes are still far below those of married couples. Like never-marrieds, they must compete with married couples who can pay more for housing, utilities, consumer goods, taxes and every other material need. They are also more likely to be raising children alone. Many divorced women must re-enter the workforce, often at the entry level, and thus have to adjust to an unforeseen, entirely new and modest lifestyle. As a result, financial, time and social pressures fill the lives of many.

It is impossible to stereotype the attitudes of divorced people. A marriage can end within months or after decades. Teenage marriages tend to be unstable, so many divorced men and women are young and childless. Mature families with growing or grown children, on the other hand, break up as well. Older divorced people's experiences are generally more traumatic; their lifestyles, attitudes and needs reflect the difference.

Nevertheless, some general traits are worth noting. Rural marriages are more stable, so rural areas have lower concentrations of divorced adults. Divorced people tend to be concentrated in cities rather than suburbs or rural areas. Our surveys find that blacks are more likely, and hispanics and Asians less likely, to be divorced than whites. Eighty-four percent of our divorced respondents live with children under the age of 13—about the same proportion as married respondents.[5]

There have always been more divorced women than men; they live longer and are less likely to remarry soon. But as the divorce rate tripled from 47 out of 1,000 adults in 1970 to 148 in 1991, the proportion of men to women evened out somewhat. In 1970, there were only 58 divorced men for every 100 divorced women. In 1991, there were 72.[6]

More than three million of these women are raising children by themselves. (Another 1.3 million women are separated, rather than divorced, and are raising children by themselves.)[7] They manage by working long hours, in most cases with little or no child support.

The lifestyles of divorced people look similar to those of never-marrieds, but with important differences. Very few divorced people are rich (despite what

Hollywood tabloids say about multimillion-dollar celebrity divorce settlements). The typical divorced person's life is modest. Seventy percent of divorced people work full-time—actually a higher rate than for either marrieds or never-marrieds. Very few—less than 5%—work part-time. A substantial number—over 20%—are unemployed.[8]

Their precarious financial status makes divorced people especially sensitive to economic change. In 1991 divorced people were more likely than the other groups to report that they were changing their spending patterns because of the weak economy: 69% were cutting back on entertainment, 65% were eating out less often and 35% were restricting their driving.[9]

Divorced adults are nearly as likely as never-marrieds, and much more likely than others, to consider themselves "stressed out." It is no wonder—they work longer hours and volunteer more of their time to nonprofit organizations and churches. In 1991, divorced people said they saw more of their family than they had the year earlier. On the other hand, they said they were seeing less of their friends, spending less time seeking education and working out less than they had been.

Values and Attitudes

Divorced men and women are different from never-marrieds in this all-important respect: they have experienced the intensities of both marriage and divorce. How do they see the world?

These experiences leave this group's values in a sort of limbo between those of never-marrieds and marrieds. For instance, divorced people consider money less important than either group. On the other hand, they value their time more. And they come close to sharing marrieds' attitudes about the importance of living comfortably, having close friends and having close family relationships.

Divorced people lie in between never-marrieds and marrieds in the confidence they express in churches, but are more negative than either in their feelings toward other authoritative institutions, such as Congress and the Supreme Court. They tend to distrust charities and nonprofits, as well as the news media and the media in general. They are especially unlikely to think that television accurately portrays the lives of Americans. The distrust of institutions they display shows them to be more alienated from public life than even never-married adults.

This group is cynical about the state of America. In 1991, 46% of them thought the country was worse off than it was a year before, compared to 37% of all other adults. Even more divorced adults thought the country would continue along its descent.

Divorced people's special circumstances uniquely shape their personal goals. Compared to the average American adult, divorced adults find close personal friendships less desirable, but value having a reputation of integrity more. They are slightly less interested in having a close relationship with God. Divorced people fall in between never-marrieds and marrieds in their desire for fame, for holding a high-paying job, for owning a large home and for involvement in a local church. Perhaps because they work such long hours, they would love not to have to work for a living. They do not particularly desire long lives. One might call them "semi-sentimental."[10]

The New Gnostics?

Fifty-eight percent of divorced adults—again, right between the proportion of never-marrieds and the proportion of marrieds—say they live by a particular philosophy of life. But their philosophies are even less shaped by religion than the philosophies of never-married adults. Divorcees tend to be more pessimistic and more individualistic, and describe themselves as "conservative" more than either marrieds or never-marrieds.

If it is true, as Harold Bloom claims,[11] that America is an increasingly gnostic country, then divorced people are leading the way. Their shattered marriages have destroyed their faith in relationships and communities, and left many of them with faith only in themselves. Three-quarters believe there is no such thing as absolute truth. Only 40% (versus 55% of all American adults) think that people should have some involvement with a religious community in order to be religious.[12]

Whether or not divorced people tend to believe in "karma" (roughly put, the idea that both good and evil actions are eventually repaid in-kind) is open to debate: they are more likely than others to hold the very common American notion that people reap what they sow. However, they are just as likely to believe, as some 96% of Americans do, that "everyone has a right to freedom and prosperity."

Eighty-seven percent of divorced people believe people are basically good—more than any other group. But these people have learned the hard way not to depend on others. Probably in reaction to the sting of their experience, over half claim that people look only after themselves. And more divorced adults than any other group think a person's first responsibility is to self.[13]

Divorcees Are Not Lonely

It is quite a surprise (and rather a mystery) that divorced people are not as likely to consider themselves lonely as are never-marrieds.[14] "Only" forty-one percent wish they had more close friends—a number that is actually lower than for any other marital category. Divorced adults are the least likely among the marital

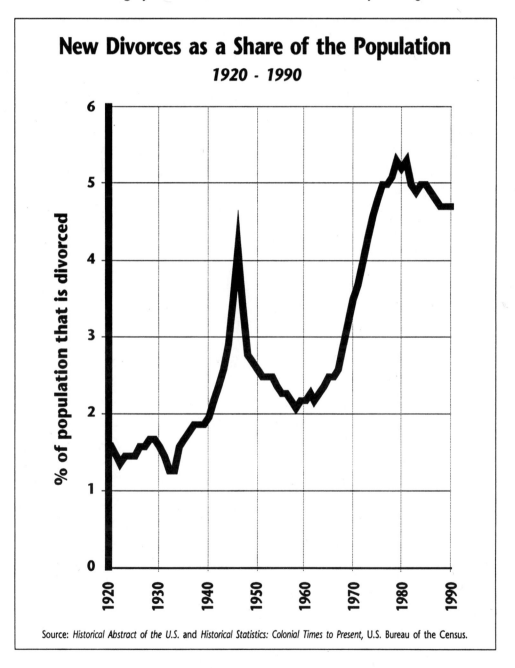

New Divorces as a Share of the Population
1920 - 1990

Source: *Historical Abstract of the U.S.* and *Historical Statistics: Colonial Times to Present*, U.S. Bureau of the Census.

subgroups to feel that they have no one to turn to for comfort and support during a crisis. Even spouses are more likely to feel alone in their times of need than are the currently divorced!

We have mentioned how the experience of divorce produces an attitude of economic and professional self-sufficiency. That self-reliance apparently extends to personal relationships as well. Divorced people answer just as often as others (that is, 70% of the time) that they find it easy to make deep, lasting friendships. Only 35%—about the average—report that they know people who are truly lonely. They feel more strongly than any other group that people are at fault if they do not make friends.[15]

Divorced people hold other interesting attitudes on relationships. While only 22% of marrieds think it is "very difficult" to keep a deep friendship with a member of the opposite sex without it becoming sexual, nearly double the share of divorced people (39%) believe it is hard for lasting friendships to stay platonic. The fragility of their former marriages and the cynicism of the singles scene may all have taken their toll.

The increasingly common experience of divorce in America has produced a unique set of people: stung by the failure of their closest relationship, they are now self-reliant and cynical about relationships in general.

Men and Women

The statistics on the numbers of divorced men and divorced women hint at substantial differences in how the two sexes experience divorce. Whether they are caused by divorce or exist beforehand, the fact remains that attitudes of divorced men and women are even more disparate than those of never-married men and divorced women.

Divorced women are more than twice as likely to feel stressed out as are divorced men—and *less likely* to see themselves as too busy. Divorced women are more likely to value close friendships, and vastly more likely to value a close relationship with God. Divorced men are lonelier than divorced women. They are more concerned with money, their careers and enjoying a comfortable life. They are more cynical about the stability of marriage. They spend more time working out and less time with friends.[16]

After a divorce, men's religious beliefs remain similar to those of women. But behaviorally, men become more career- and money-oriented; women become more relationship-oriented. It is relatively easy to explain this change. After a

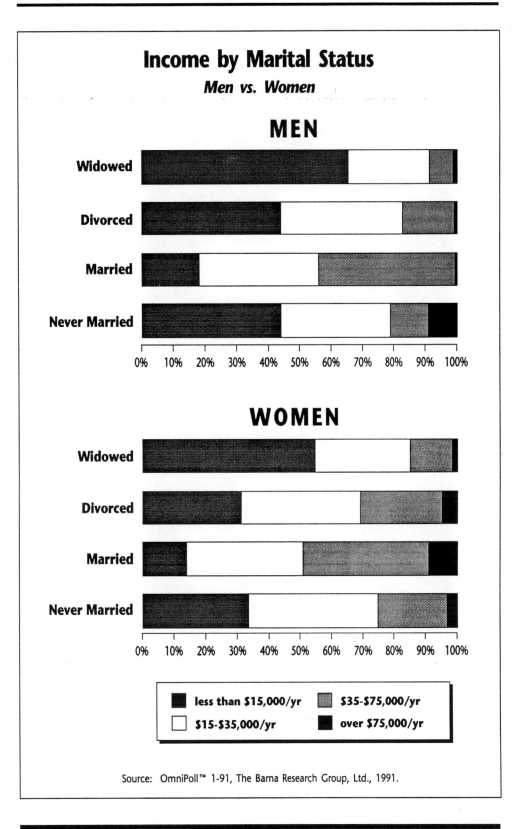

Source: OmniPoll™ 1-91, The Barna Research Group, Ltd., 1991.

divorce, men's lives usually become simpler. Even if their income drops, their expenses tend to decline. They are emotionally affected by the experience, but tend to channel their frustrations into their careers. Men are more likely to remarry than divorced women, and they do so earlier, as well.[17]

In comparison, women's lives become much more complicated. If there were children from the marriage, women usually retain custody of the young ones. Their incomes shrink drastically. Reentering the labor force, perhaps after years of being a housewife, can be intimidating and discouraging. Divorced women may need to return to school for job training, to buy new wardrobes, or to spend money on any number of other items required to prepare for their new lives. Divorce is a more traumatic and life-changing experience for women, especially women who sacrificed their financial and personal independence years earlier in order to raise their now-broken families.

Some poverty experts describe the long-term effects of divorce and out-of-wedlock childbearing as "the feminization of poverty." It is obvious that both men and women suffer substantially from divorce. But for women, the suffering is often greater, lasts longer and is more likely to be permanent.

The First Year, The Worst Year

The transition from a marriage back to an unmarried lifestyle is a tremendous shock. Some experts liken the trauma immediately following the death of a person's marriage to the grieving process that follows the death of a loved one.

The first year is the worst year. Legal and financial skirmishes worsen the already intense personal stresses. Relationships with family, friends and workmates change. One survey of recently divorced adults found that in the first year following marriage, divorced men and women:

- usually drink and smoke more than when married.

- may experience difficulty sleeping.

- have higher energy levels.

- work harder and earn more (though many women are starting from an artificially low base).

- commonly experience depression.

- usually increase, but occasionally decrease, their sexual activity.

- report more sexual problems.

- often lose weight, though they occasionally gain weight.

- often become happier, but occasionally become unhappier.

- tend to become healthier and increase in self-respect.

- may get along better with their families and children (but occasionally, relationships worsen).

- tend to report personal growth.[18]

The surveyors reported that the people they interviewed were often amazed that they were feeling such a wide range of emotions, ranging from euphoria to depression. They felt as unprepared for the emotional change as they were for the lifestyle change that divorce brought on. From the perspective of the others in their lives, these people felt a variety of feelings and experienced a set of needs that turned out to be quite different from what they would have expected.[19]

It can be as difficult for divorced people themselves to understand what is happening as it is for the people around them. It is worth keeping these surprises in mind when trying to understand the erratic behavior that can immediately follow a divorce.

Divorcees With Children

Most divorced people are parents. So, at least for a while, most of them become single parents. They have a different perspective than other Americans: they know more than any other group how hard a road single parenthood can be.

Nine out of ten divorced adults personally know at least one single parent. About the same number think it is more difficult for single parents to raise children than for married couples.[20]

But there is more to the story than simply the hardships of single parenthood. Divorced parents see the task as tougher than never-married parents do. In fact, 78% "strongly" see it that way, compared to two-thirds of marrieds and widows and only 54% of never-marrieds.[21]

This figure, which is high compared to that for never-marrieds (many of whom are parents), suggests that divorced people find their lives as single parents unusually difficult. There are several possible reasons for their feelings, each having important consequences. First, divorced people's lives may actually be harder. The shock of their lifestyle change, the trauma of divorce, the financial loss and their worries for their children all make the task of being an effective parent even more difficult than it would have been already. Second, they can draw upon both their married and divorced experiences in formulating their opinions about single parenthood. Never-married parents have never known the comparative ease of raising children in a two-parent family and have not had to adjust between the two lifestyles. They may be less intimidated about raising children on their own, not having known any other way of life.

Divorced people's attitudes on raising their families are surprisingly complex. They reflect a mixture of pride, frustration and defensiveness. For instance, though the overwhelming majority of divorced adults think raising children alone is more difficult than in a two-parent family, only about 40% think children of single parents are put at a disadvantage. Well over half (62%) feel single-parent families are "no different" from any other type of family, except for the absence of one adult in the home.[22]

Divorced people have vivid and lingering memories of marriage, and those memories are good as well as bad. Only one-third of all divorced men and women think remarriage is the best answer. Yet they express views on the roles of husbands and wives that are surprisingly traditional. Seventy-two percent think families are most likely to be happy when mothers stay at home. Only 27% think it makes no difference which parent stays home to care for the children; almost all of the rest think the mother should be the caregiver. Over two-thirds—more than any other category except widows—feel families are more likely to be content when the family sacrifices financially to enable a parent to stay home rather than putting the children in day-care. Divorced people (along with most other Americans) strongly believe that having traditional families makes child-raising an easier and more productive experience.[23]

These views may be in part a reaction by people who have experienced nontraditional ways of raising families—either by choice or because of circumstances beyond their control—and have found them inadequate. Yet at the same time, divorced adults show some defensiveness about their performance as single parents. They deny that living in a single-parent home penalizes children or marks their families as abnormal, saying in effect that they can get along by themselves just fine, thank you. Divorcees feel great pride along with their fatigue in their accomplishments as single parents.[24]

How Divorcees See Marriage

Two-thirds of divorced people describe their lifestyles as "traditional." This is a surprisingly high number, because by any objective criterion, their lives are untraditional. There is no precedent for 150-in-1,000 divorce rates in the American or Judeo-Christian traditions.

This anomaly can be explained by considering that most people define their lives in terms of the people around them, not people in the past. More and more Americans are divorced. Therefore, they reason, more and more of them lead traditional lives.

Their thinking may be flawed, but it has the healthy side-effect of reducing the alienation from the mainstream one might expect divorced people to feel. Seven divorced people in eight affirm that they are part of families.[25]

Just what do they mean? Divorced adults' definitions of family should probably be considered "semi-traditional." Seventy-three percent of them—less than never-marrieds, but more than marrieds—consider cohabiters with children to be "families." Only 20%—the same as marrieds, and fewer than never-marrieds—consider a same-sex relationship a family. And nearly 90%—the same as nearly every other people group—consider single-parent households to be families.[26]

Some attitudes betray the frustrations that divorced people feel about their new lives. As the previous section has shown, divorced people consider traditional families the best place to rear children. Divorcees believe even more strongly than spouses do that marriage should be a permanent arrangement. Two-thirds consider the permanence of marriage divinely ordained. About the same number believe that marriage is a prerequisite for a stable family. Yet nearly half, more than in any other group, call a successful marriage "almost impossible" to attain. No other group considers marriage as central to a successful family. Yet no other group considers it as unattainable.[27]

In most of their attitudes towards raising children, divorced adults resemble marrieds more than never-marrieds. They are skeptical of full-time day care for children. They believe in the greater value of "quality time" with children. And they would give churches a lot of responsibility for teaching values to children, rather than schools. Divorced adults are similar to marrieds in their reluctance to give the media or other children peers much responsibility for values education.

Like spouses, 90% of divorced people believe children who are raised by their married, natural parents will have successful upbringings. But one-third of them—more than other groups—think that parents who stay unhappily married to protect their children are doing so in vain. They are far more optimistic about the future of children who live with a parent who divorces and either remarries or stays unmarried.[28]

Good Times, Bad Times

When asked what personal relationship they now find most satisfying, divorced men and women tend to answer "their children" or their "best friend." Fewer mention parents or relatives. Men are more likely to mention friends, while women are much more likely to mention blood relatives.

Many divorced people tend to be loners. While people in all other marital categories are more likely to spend their free time with others, half of divorced adults say that they usually spend theirs by themselves. They tend to go out with friends (half of men, 30% of women) and children (15%, evenly split), rather than other relatives (6%). In contrast, half of all never-marrieds go out with friends; one-third spend most of their free time alone and one-sixth spend their free time with their parents. If divorced people feel family ties, they seem to act on them less often than others—even people who have never married.[29]

Finally, marriage has lost some—but not all—of its appeal to divorced people. Over half of divorced adults are interested in remarrying under the right circumstances. If they had it to do over, one-quarter would actually have married the same person. Over one-third would have married another. About the same number would have stayed single, and about half say they would have cohabited. When asked what divorced people found most satisfying about their marriages, the most common replies involve children (one in three) and companionship (one in four). One in seven say they cannot recall anything satisfying. Their recollections of bad experiences involve negative opinions of their spouses (one in four), followed by poor communication, alcoholism and finances.[30]

Divorced people's predictions on the future of marriage are mixed. Two-thirds expect new laws giving adults even more freedom on marriage and family matters. They have more faith than other groups do that marriage will not be replaced by cohabitation. Despite their cynicism about marital stability and personal experience, 40% of divorced people believe most new marriages will last five years or more. That is not exactly cheerleading, but it is no more pessimistic than the view of never-marrieds.[31]

In the opinion of this group, marriage is down—but not out.

The Confusing Cohabiters

Divorced people's attitudes toward cohabitation are full of surprises. When asked whether it is best for partners to live together before marrying, only 42% agree.[32]

Yet over half of all divorced adults who remarry cohabit between their marriages.[33] Divorced people who live together are much less likely to wish to marry than never-marrieds who live together[34]—yet they are much more likely to marry.[35] In fact, two-thirds of recent remarriages were preceded by cohabitation.[36] Finally, remarriage rates for women, especially for women with older children, declined rapidly during the 1960s and '70s.

How can findings this seemingly contradictory be untangled?

It is important to start by understanding that not all divorced adults behave the same way. Marriage and divorce statistics are often distorted by the fact that some

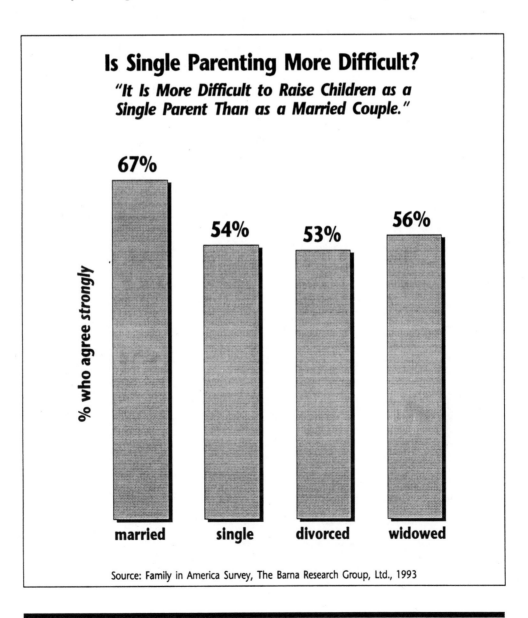

Is Single Parenting More Difficult?
"It Is More Difficult to Raise Children as a Single Parent Than as a Married Couple."

67%   54%   53%   56%

% who agree strongly

married   single   divorced   widowed

Source: Family in America Survey, The Barna Research Group, Ltd., 1993

people marry and divorce many times. Theirs are a disproportionate percentage of the fragile marriages.

Consider this hypothetical example: a woman marries and divorces three times; another three women marry but never divorce. Taken together, these four people have experienced six marriages and three divorces. Yet three of the four have stable marriages. The 50% "failure rate" can lead observers to think that marriage is *less stable* in this group than it really is. And the "remarriage rate" of 67% (three divorces, two remarriages) suggests a *more stable* remarriage rate than really exists.

So to some extent the weird numbers reflect several subgroups of divorce adults with different attitudes and behaviors. Divorced men behave differently and remarry at different rates. Some people go through multiple marriages and divorces, cohabiting in-between. And a substantial number of divorced people neither believe in nor engage in cohabitation. Furthermore, divorcées in more mature families, who are more financially independent today than they once were, may elect not to remarry at all and become, for want of a better term, "divorce widows." Within the single category of "the divorced" are actually several disparate groups. They share different ideas about the depth of commitment required in marriage and the value of cohabitation. One group might indeed be called "traditional" in the true sense of the word: despite, or perhaps because of being divorced, they are reluctant to shed their strongly held views of the necessity of a stable marriage.

So why the gap between intentions and behavior? One hypothesis is worth pondering: many people may begin living together instead of remarrying and risking divorce. Once cohabiting, many people are drawn into marriage anyway.

How Divorced People See the Church

Divorced people exhibit the same curious mixture of respect, involvement and detachment toward the church that they do towards families and other institutions. Unraveling the Gordian knot of attitudes yields some interesting information.

These people are nearest never-marrieds in their degree of church involvement, and closest to marrieds in their religious beliefs and private religious practices.[37] They are a bit more likely than never-marrieds to have recently attended a church worship service, religious instruction, class or church-related small group. But they are almost as likely as marrieds to have read a Bible recently, to have prayed to God or to have shared their religious beliefs with someone of different beliefs.[38]

Two-thirds of currently divorced adults desire a close relationship with God.[39] And almost 70% of divorced people say they have made a "personal commitment to Jesus Christ that is still important" in their lives—about the same share as that of marrieds and decidedly greater than that of non-marrieds (only 54%).[40] Of

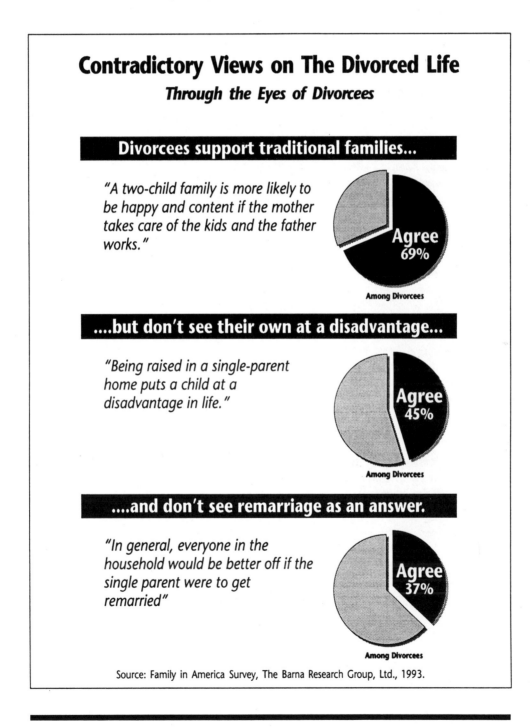

Contradictory Views on The Divorced Life
Through the Eyes of Divorcees

Divorcees support traditional families...

"A two-child family is more likely to be happy and content if the mother takes care of the kids and the father works."

Agree 69%

Among Divorcees

....but don't see their own at a disadvantage...

"Being raised in a single-parent home puts a child at a disadvantage in life."

Agree 45%

Among Divorcees

....and don't see remarriage as an answer.

"In general, everyone in the household would be better off if the single parent were to get remarried"

Agree 37%

Among Divorcees

Source: Family in America Survey, The Barna Research Group, Ltd., 1993.

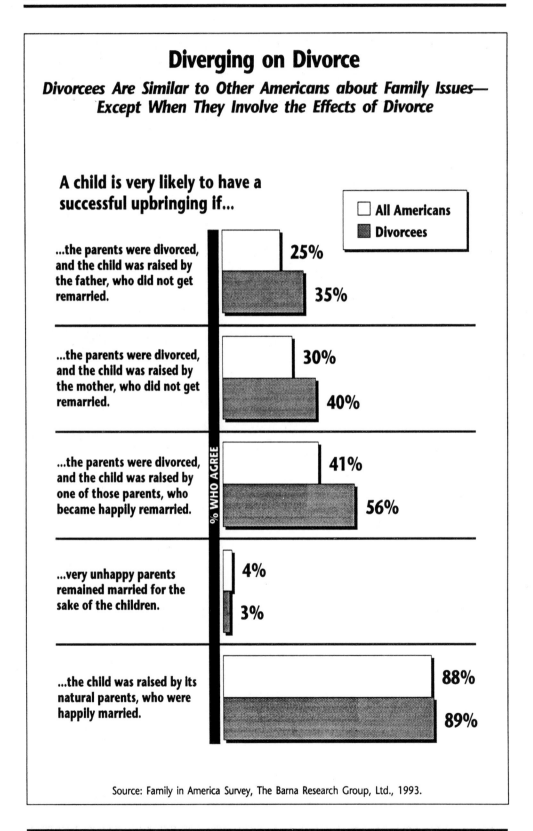

Diverging on Divorce

Divorcees Are Similar to Other Americans about Family Issues—
Except When They Involve the Effects of Divorce

A child is very likely to have a successful upbringing if...

Legend:
☐ All Americans
■ Divorcees

...the parents were divorced, and the child was raised by the father, who did not get remarried.
All Americans: 25%
Divorcees: 35%

...the parents were divorced, and the child was raised by the mother, who did not get remarried.
All Americans: 30%
Divorcees: 40%

...the parents were divorced, and the child was raised by one of those parents, who became happily remarried.
All Americans: 41%
Divorcees: 56%

...very unhappy parents remained married for the sake of the children.
All Americans: 4%
Divorcees: 3%

...the child was raised by its natural parents, who were happily married.
All Americans: 88%
Divorcees: 89%

(% WHO AGREE)

Source: Family in America Survey, The Barna Research Group, Ltd., 1993.

those people, two-thirds believe people go to heaven because they accept Christ as their Savior and confess their sins. That is more than any other group, including widows—the people that, as we shall see in Chapter Seven, spoil the curve for all the rest on spiritual matters.

The importance divorced people give religion in their lives falls in between those of marrieds and of never-marrieds. Seventy-seven percent of divorced adults (compared to 64% of never-marrieds) think the Bible has practical advice for unmarried adults. But divorced adults attribute no more religious influence on their own views of family, marriage, childrearing and sex than other groups.

Divorced people generally have positive opinions of major Christian denominations. They come close to marrieds in their appreciation of them, and are definitely more positive than are never-marrieds. They also display positive assessments of Protestant churches' sensitivities toward the needs of single parents. Over half thought churches to be very or somewhat sensitive.[41]

So why do divorced people's religious attitudes and religious practices not match? Why does church involvement not reflect church enthusiasm? And what does it mean for church leaders?

Explaining the Gap

Remember how busy divorced people's schedules are, and how their divorces continue to rock their financial, family, career and personal lives? All of these stresses make it difficult to become involved in organizations that place a lot of demands on a person's time—like church.

But there are other reasons for their inactivity. Divorced people are generally turned off by organized institutions. Nine out of ten once attended church regularly.[42] But only about one-fifth now think a person must be at least somewhat involved with a church or other religious organization in order to be "religious."[43] There is no strong link between this group's private religion and its public religion.

Divorced people's preferences in church services usually match those of other Americans, particularly other unmarrieds. However, this group is different in several ways. Divorced adults are slightly more likely to prefer larger churches, churches with Sunday morning and midweek evening services, and churches that focus their attention on the needs of their members, rather than on those of others in the community or of people overseas. Divorced people, along with never-marrieds, are especially likely to prefer services with some traditional and some contemporary music, rather than simply one or the other.[44]

From the standpoint of the church, divorced people are an intriguing and challenging group to try to serve. Their lack of church involvement may make them appear to be alienated or hostile to religion in general. But their private religious practices—frequent Bible reading, regular religious television and radio exposure and dedication to prayer—show that they are far from being a "lost

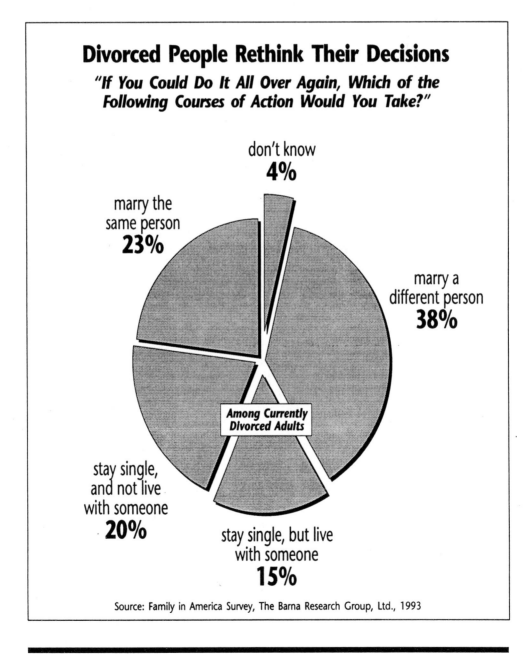

Divorced People Rethink Their Decisions

"If You Could Do It All Over Again, Which of the Following Courses of Action Would You Take?"

don't know
4%

marry the same person
23%

marry a different person
38%

Among Currently Divorced Adults

stay single, and not live with someone
20%

stay single, but live with someone
15%

Source: Family in America Survey, The Barna Research Group, Ltd., 1993

cause." And divorced people are extremely needy people. Philosophically, they are more in tune with the church than their cousins, the never-married. Their schedules and temperaments mean that churches that are creative and take the time to understand divorced adults' unique attitudes, lifestyles and needs will stand the best chances of serving them and making them a part of their communities.

These people exist in a kind of halfway house between those of never-marrieds and currently married couples. They are an anomaly, a part of Unmarried America all to themselves that deserves special attention from the church.

N   O   T   E   S

1 *Statistical Abstract of the United States 1992*, p. 44.

2 Popenoe, David, "Flight from the Nuclear Family: Trends of the Past Three Decades," *Public Perspective* (March-April 1991).

3 *Statistical Abstract of the United States 1992*, p. 44.

4 U.S. Bureau of the Census, *Money Income of Households, Families, and Persons in the United States: 1991* (Washington, DC: U.S. Government Printing Office, 1992), p. 112.

5 Barna Research Group, Ltd., OmniPoll™ 2-91.

6 *Statistical Abstract of the United States 1992*, p. 44.

7 *Child Support and Alimony: 1989.*

8 Barna Research Group, Ltd., Family in America survey, 1992.

9 Barna Research Group, Ltd., OmniPoll™ 1-91.

10 Barna Research Group, Ltd., OmniPoll™ 1-91.

11 Bloom, Harold, *The American Religion: The Emergence of the Post-Christian Nation* (New York: Simon and Schuster, 1992).

12 Barna Research Group, Ltd., OmniPoll™ 1-91.

13 Barna Research Group, Ltd., OmniPoll™ 2-91.

14 Ibid.

15 Barna Research Group, Ltd., OmniPoll™ 1-91 and OmniPoll™ 2-91.

16 Ibid.

17 Ibid.

18 Simenauer, Jacqueline and David Carroll, *Singles* (New York: Simon and Schuster, 1982), pp. 371-399.

19   Ibid.

20   Barna Research Group, Ltd., Family in America survey.

21   Ibid.

22   Ibid.

23   Ibid.

24   Barna Research Group, Ltd., Family in America survey.

25   Ibid.

26   Ibid.

27   Ibid.

28   Ibid.

29   Ibid.

30   Ibid.

31   Ibid.

32   Family in America survey.

33   *Young Adults' Views of Marriage, Cohabitation, and Family*, p. 1.

34   Ibid., p. 8.

35   Ibid., pp. 4-5.

36   Ibid., p. 5

37   Barna Research Group, Ltd., OmniPoll™ 1-91.

38   Barna Research Group, Ltd., Family in America survey.

39   Barna Research Group, Ltd., OmniPoll™ 1-91.

40   Barna Research Group, Ltd., Family in America survey.

41   Barna Research Group, Ltd., OmniPoll™ 2-91.

42   Barna Research Group, Ltd., Unchurched survey.

43   Barna Research Group, Ltd., OmniPoll™ 1-91.

44   Barna Research Group, Ltd., OmniPoll™ 2-91.

C H A P T E R   S E V E N

The Church Ladies

*T*he career of Dana Carvey (*Saturday Night Live's* President Bush and shy headbanger Garth of *Wayne's World* and forthcoming *Wayne's World II*) first took off with his portrayal of The Church Lady, America's greatest Satan-basher and crusader for traditional values since the '80s' fallen televangelists. You don't want to mess with the Church Lady. She owns the moral high ground, and is fooled by no one. One smirk and a "Well, isn't that *special!*" and her opponent is *history.*

The Church Lady may seem like an unfair way to characterize the last group in Unmarried America—the widows. But behind the caricature lie traits that really do characterize America's widows: firm morality, respect for and deep involvement in great American institutions, and a powerful conviction that no matter how far people wander, no matter how long it takes, someday they will be back.

There are Church Ladies all over the world. Consider the widows who kept Russian Orthodoxy alive during its decades under Communist rule. The widows—those who remembered the Church as it had been, and who had the least to lose by staying involved—braved the persecution, kept the faith alive and taught it to millions of grandchildren. Who is foolish enough to argue with a Russian *babooshka* (or, for that matter, her American counterpart)? Today, the *babooshkas* are vindicated: the children they taught in secret fill Russia's churches once again.

Widows are a tremendously influential group of Americans. They pour time, money and energy into churches, nonprofit organizations, schools and political parties. They are a backbone of tradition both in America's churches and in American society as a whole. This dedication has its weaknesses as well as its strengths, as we shall see.

Widows' Vital Statistics

The fact that women live longer than men shapes the demographics of American widows. (We shall call them "widows" because they are primarily women, but our findings are based on samples of both widows and widowers.) Twelve percent of American women, and 3% of American men, survive their spouses and remain unmarried. About one-quarter of all Americans ages 65-74 and about half of all Americans over age 75 are widows. They total almost 14 million Americans.[1] One-third of women from 65-74 years of age are widows, while fewer than 10% of men of that age are widowers. Two out of three women over 75, but only one in four men over 75, are widowed.

Widows' statistics look distinct from those of either marrieds or other unmarrieds. Most widows, and most other elderly unmarrieds, live alone,[2] though a few live with one or more of their children. Many more live in the country or the suburbs than live in the city. Because they are older, they tend to be less educated. They have by far the lowest incomes among all the groups studied here. Over 80% are unemployed.[3]

Whereas the elderly were formerly cared for in their twilight years by family or the church, things are different today. Churches have generally removed themselves from the elderly care business. Family members pretty much followed suit – especially when the adults who would have to provide care for aging parents are Baby Boomers. The degree of lifestyle sacrifice required from Boomers to care for their parents adequately is just too much: they would rather provide financially for their parents to live in a retirement community or nursing home than give up their own time, space and emotional energy for their parents.

The New Elderly

One look at the grim expressions on nineteenth-century photographic portraits is enough to show how low the quality of life for America's elderly was until recently. Our great-great-grandparents could not have imagined life for senior citizens as it now is. Today older adults smile in their photos, and for good reason. Seniors—widows included—are much better off materially than their ancestors.

The numbers reveal the revolution in the lives of America's elderly that has occurred in the last few decades. Life expectancy at birth for people born from 1878 to 1882—people who would have become senior citizens in the 1940's—was 41.7 years for men and 43.5 years for women. But for men and women born between 1929 and 1931—who are becoming senior citizens in the 1990's—life expectancy at birth was 59.3 years and 62.6 years, respectively.[4] About three-quarters of this change was due to decreased infant and child mortality; nevertheless, by the time they reached adulthood, the latter generation could expect to live more than five years longer than the former generation. As a result of increased longevity, a far greater proportion of Americans is elderly today than 50 years ago. An individual can expect not only to live long enough to become a senior citizen, but to spend more of his or her life *as* a senior citizen.

Between these two eras, incomes increased so much that life after retirement became a more pleasing prospect. Per capita income more than doubled between 1940 and 1970.[5] People could save for their "golden years" and support retirement lifestyles that involved active social lives, recreation and travel, and greater comfort and luxury.

What about those too poor to save for retirement? They actually constituted most of America's poor in 1940. That year, less than $500,000 in old-age, survivors, disability and health insurance was paid to widows and widowers. Social Security and a host of other transfer payment programs changed this picture dramatically. By 1970, over $4 billion was being spent every year on social insurance for the elderly.[6] If older Americans are not filthy rich, they are no longer filthy poor, either.

So meet the new class of elderly Americans. They are less likely to have been widowed at a young age and left with the responsibility of raising children in single-parent homes. They enjoy higher life expectancies. Their increased wealth and the availability of government benefits have given them lives of relative comfort. In short, by any historical standard, they *are* living in a sort of Golden Age for seniors.

But this is not the whole story. Over this time, the nuclear family continued to replace the extended family. Today, elderly Americans are generally expected to take care of themselves. They look less to their children for support and more to their own retirement planning strategies. They expect to live not with their children but by themselves, in special communities for seniors or in rest homes. Although their incomes are typically higher, their expenses are also *much* higher. They bear the brunt of increased medical care costs, and fear that inflation will wipe out the proceeds from the money they have worked to save. The economic gains of the last few decades have been accompanied by the emergence of an entirely new set of lifestyles for elderly Americans.

The lives of widows have been touched just as dramatically by these changes. In fact, the precarious financial status of many widows has made them even *more* sensitive to the increased expenses of their new lifestyle than married seniors. Elderly unmarrieds are more likely to be poor than elderly married people, and elderly women are more likely to be poor than elderly men. Unmarried elderly women, the largest of the four subgroups, are also the most likely of America's elderly to be poor.[7]

Divorced People, or Widows?

A proportion of men and women, particularly those that are older, choose not to remarry after their divorces. Are they to remain "divorced people" for the rest of their lives, even though their attitudes and lifestyles are really closer to those of widows? For instance, some Census categories treat divorced adults as widows only after their ex-spouses die. Is this a valid dividing line?

Forces like this that cloud the statistical waters and challenge our most basic assumptions about Americans are not yet the problem they will be someday, since the oldest cohort of Americans came from families formed before the "divorce revolution." Nevertheless, the proportion of divorced adults over 65 doubled from 2.3% in 1980 to 5% in 1990.[8] In the years to come, expect the numbers of unmarried seniors to rise dramatically due to the aging of divorced people, and the numbers of unmarried men to rise even more dramatically. Expect lifestyles and attitudes to change as the proportion of elderly men to elderly women changes and as elderly subcultures begin to reflect the values that characterize divorced men and women as well as married couples. Also, since divorced people tend to be poorer than marrieds, and have fewer years in which to save for retirement, expect the rates of elderly poverty to increase, perhaps substantially. Their greater numbers and needs may place an unexpected burden on public assistance programs for the elderly which are already expected to be overwhelmed by the sheer numbers of aging Americans.

We do not yet know how the influx of divorced elderly people will change the traditional ways of elderly America. But it is safe to predict that the change that has swept the young will invade the top age bracket too, with unpredictable results.

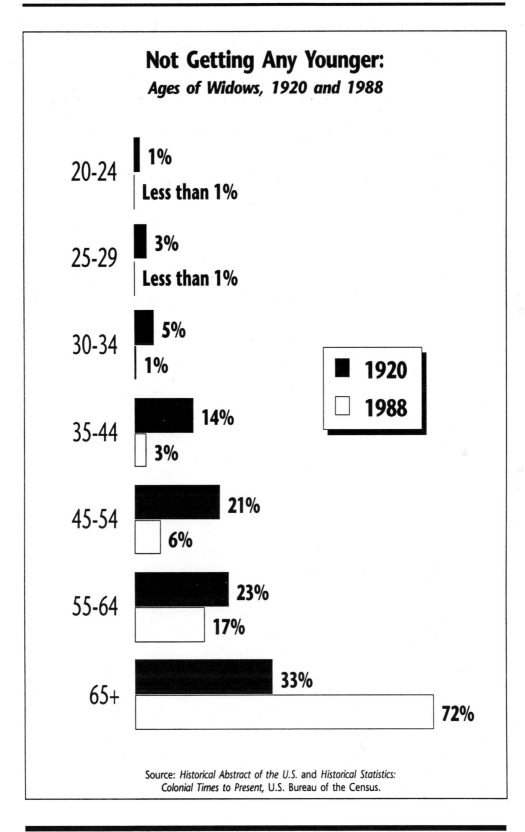

Not Getting Any Younger:
Ages of Widows, 1920 and 1988

Age	1920	1988
20-24	1%	Less than 1%
25-29	3%	Less than 1%
30-34	5%	1%
35-44	14%	3%
45-54	21%	6%
55-64	23%	17%
65+	33%	72%

■ 1920
□ 1988

Source: *Historical Abstract of the U.S.* and *Historical Statistics: Colonial Times to Present,* U.S. Bureau of the Census.

The Way Widows See the World

On nearly every issue we analyze, widows give the most traditional responses of any marital group. Widows support marriage, support the family, support the church and predict a return to more traditional times. Though the experience of widowhood changes the lives and some of the beliefs of widows, other attitudes seem untouched. In many areas, widows' views are about as traditional as those of their married contemporaries. On the other hand, some of their attitudes do not fit the widow stereotype.

Widows are more likely to describe themselves as politically conservative and traditional than are people in other marital categories, including marrieds. They spend their time with friends, children, neighbors and church acquaintances. Widows find relationships with their children the most satisfying in their lives. However, some widows find relationships with friends, other relatives and even neighbors more satisfying.[9]

There is a lot of free time in a typical widow's schedule. This has benefits, not the least of which is that widows are much less likely than never-marrieds, marrieds or divorced people to describe themselves as "stressed out." Surprisingly, despite their extensive free time, widows are no more likely to describe themselves as lonely than any other group of unmarrieds.[10]

Widows spend their leisure time reading and watching television, watching or involved in sports, going out socially, doing yard and garden work, working with crafts, enjoying arts and music and playing games. They usually do these things alone or with friends, whom widows value very highly.[11] This contrasts dramatically with married couples, who are much more likely to enjoy sports, spending time with family and reading, but who do not consider tasks like yard work enjoyable activities. Married adults recreate with their spouses or their children more often than they do alone or with friends.[12]

Widows are big believers in public schools, churches and the military, but are no more likely than the general population to trust many organizations, such as Congress, the Supreme Court, hospitals, the media, charities and private business. Volunteerism is a time-honored way for widows to stay personally active and involved in their communities. About as many widows as marrieds volunteer to help non-church organizations, and widows more than any others volunteer their time for—you guessed it—churches.[13]

Like marrieds and divorced people, widows tend to consider money to be only moderately important. (Never-marrieds are the only group that considers money especially important.) The key difference is the way widows use their money. Widows see their money as helping to secure a comfortable life, not becoming members of the "rich and famous." Perhaps because of their already frugal lifestyles, widows were less likely to report that they were changing their spending patterns to help them weather the 1991 recession.

Along with marrieds and divorced adults, widows value both family and their health very highly. Their desires are much more family-, friend- and God-centered than those of marrieds or other unmarrieds. Fame, influence, high-paying jobs and leisure hold little allure. In this respect, widows are the exact opposite of their

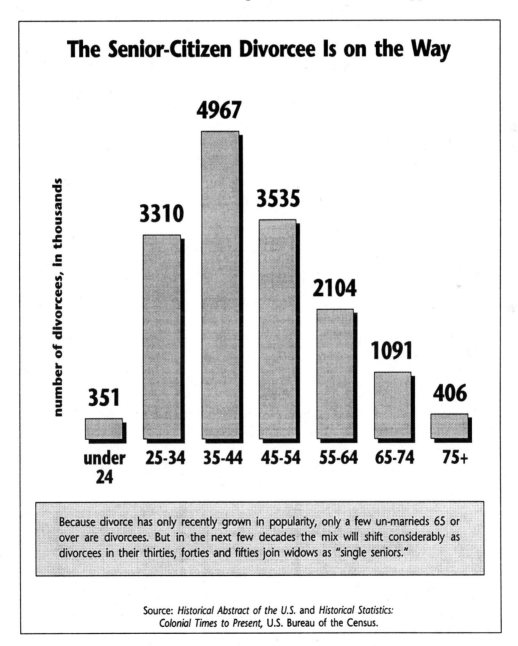

The Senior-Citizen Divorcee Is on the Way

number of divorcees, in thousands

351 — under 24
3310 — 25-34
4967 — 35-44
3535 — 45-54
2104 — 55-64
1091 — 65-74
406 — 75+

Because divorce has only recently grown in popularity, only a few un-marrieds 65 or over are divorcees. But in the next few decades the mix will shift considerably as divorcees in their thirties, forties and fifties join widows as "single seniors."

Source: *Historical Abstract of the U.S.* and *Historical Statistics: Colonial Times to Present*, U.S. Bureau of the Census.

never-married counterparts. And, surprisingly, widows value their time quite a bit. More than one-quarter say they are "too busy." They consider free time even more important than other groups do.

Rugged Communitarians

Even though widows' values are communal, they value self-reliance. They are more likely than other Americans to believe that their "first responsibility" is to themselves.[14]

This attitude does not exist in a vacuum. Widows tend to be lonely, and do not enjoy extensive contacts with family as do their married contemporaries. They are more likely than either divorced or never-married people to believe that in times of trouble, they have no one to turn to for comfort or support.[15] Widows learn from experience that they need to make friendships and get involved on their own initiative. They believe that people have no one to blame but themselves if they fail to make friends. Widows tend to believe that the axiom "you reap what you sow" is true, and they sow accordingly. To make the friends they consider so important, widows look to church and to community organizations. The image of the lonely widow relying on her children for contact with the outside world is only partly true. Many widows live those kinds of lives. But many others become involved, develop friendships and live active lives apart from their relatives.

It is interesting that self-reliance is a value shared by both widowed and divorced people: the similarities between the two groups indicate that at least some of the changes in attitudes divorced people experience are in response not to the trauma of their divorces, but to their new-found independence.

Widows and Families

Widows tend to have strong, positive views on the American family. This is a result of two factors. First, their age group shares a stronger commitment to marriage and experiences much lower rates of divorce and single-parenthood. Second, they typically feel they had successful marriages themselves, unions which ended only by the deaths of their spouses.

Almost all widows—more than either never-marrieds or divorced people—consider themselves to be part of a family. And when widows say "family," they do not have alternative family models in mind. Fewer than half of all widows consider a couple who lives together and has children a "family," compared to 72% of all American adults. Widows are also less inclined to consider same-sex lovers who live together a family. On the other hand, widows join the vast majority of other Americans who consider single parents raising children to be families.[16]

Many widows are surprisingly pessimistic about the future of families. The vast majority believe marriage is a prerequisite to a strong family, and more widows than any other marital group believe that marriage is an institution that is ordained by God and meant to last a lifetime. But widows are more likely than

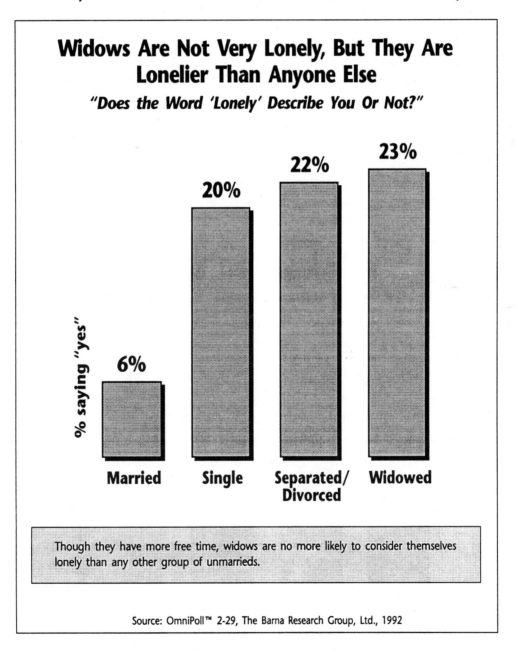

Widows Are Not Very Lonely, But They Are Lonelier Than Anyone Else

"Does the Word 'Lonely' Describe You Or Not?"

% saying "yes"

6%	20%	22%	23%
Married	Single	Separated/ Divorced	Widowed

Though they have more free time, widows are no more likely to consider themselves lonely than any other group of unmarrieds.

Source: OmniPoll™ 2-29, The Barna Research Group, Ltd., 1992

the average American to believe it is "almost impossible" to have a successful marriage today. About half think that most people who get married will divorce within five years. One-third (compared to only 20% of marrieds) think that raising children now is less fun than it used to be.[17]

A minority of widows—but a larger minority than in any other marital group—thinks marriage is outdated and no longer fits into American culture. These people do not see marriage returning to the status it enjoyed during the "Good Old Days."

This is another area of commonality between divorced people and widows. Both groups see value in marriage and wish marriage in America were in better shape than it is. But they are skeptical that it ever will be. The two groups consider the Cleaver family model a wonderful remnant of the past, but a remnant of the past nonetheless.

Still, there are important differences. Where divorced people do not support tougher divorce laws as a way to improve marriages, widows do. And where divorced people are as supportive as other Americans of the idea of cohabiting as a way to pre-test a marriage, widows disagree. They prefer traditional family arrangements where parents are married, where parents teach values to children and where a church is in a position of influence. They overwhelmingly prefer households where the father works and the mother raises the children, even if it means financial sacrifice. Widows do not share divorced people's optimism about the future of children who grow up with divorced parents who do not remarry. But they are more optimistic than others about the future of adopted children who live with happily married couples.[18]

Most widows are elderly. Their generation supports the social mores that, in their opinion, worked pretty well for them. And, though they see a dimmer future for families than do other marital groups, half of today's widows see an eventual resurgence of the traditional family values of the '50s. In their minds, what worked for them will someday work again.

Widows and the Church

"Do not take advantage of a widow or an orphan. If you do and they cry out to me, I will certainly hear their cry." (Exodus 22:22-23 NIV)

"Give proper recognition to the widows who are really in need." (1 Timothy 5:1 NIV)

"Religion that God our Father accepts as pure and faultless is this: to look after orphans and widows in their distress and to keep oneself from being polluted by the world." (James 1:27, NIV)

Widows have always been one of God's chief concerns. And in twentieth century America, the feeling is mutual. No other sector of the population has as much respect for the Christian church as do our widows.

In biblical times, no one was as helpless as widows and orphans. In an economy where people worked hard for subsistence earnings and often died at a comparatively young age, to be a widow or an orphan was a far more precarious life than it is today. God looked after them, so the church looked after them, too.

Since widows enjoy better lives today than they did then, they have a different relationship with the church. Now, widows are probably better known for being supporters of churches than for being their beneficiaries. Nevertheless, many are in need, and many churches assist them much as they did nearly two thousand years ago. Regular church programs for seniors like Meals on Wheels are common, as are special efforts after disasters. For instance, many local ministries provided food, water and batteries to shut-ins after the Los Angeles riots.

The relationship is obviously changing. What do widows think about the church and about Christianity?

About nine in 10 widows describe themselves as Christians—a greater proportion than that of marrieds, divorced people and never-marrieds. The clear majority of widows say that religion has influenced their personal philosophies and their thinking on sex, marriage, childrearing and family issues. Over three-quarters believe the Bible has practical advice both on life as a single adult and on life within a family. No other marital group has a higher opinion of Christianity's relevance to the world.[19]

Widows do not just think a lot *of* Christianity; they think a lot *about* Christianity. Over four-fifths desire a close relationship with God.[20] Three-quarters describe religion as "very important" in their lives. Nearly as many say they have made a personal commitment to Jesus Christ that remains important to them. Over three-quarters of widows express confidence in Christian churches. In a typical week, more than half of all widows go to a church service; more than half read the Bible away from church; one-third attend a Bible or religious study class; more than 90% pray to God; and nearly one-third share their beliefs with someone of different beliefs.[21] No other marital group shares these attitudes and commitments so intensely.

These happy statistics do not mean homogeneity, though. Nearly nine in ten widows responded in one of our surveys that they considered people "basically good." Six in ten considered Satan merely a metaphor for evil. And over half did not believe in absolute truth. While many widows believe a person goes to heaven because of confessing one's sins as well as confessing Christ as one's savior, others believe God saves everyone, or believe salvation comes by trying to obey the Ten Commandments. Still others do not know what happens when a person dies.[22]

For this group, religion fits into a broader cultural outlook. Widows like their churches traditional. They prefer denominational churches and like their services to be held in traditional church buildings and on Sunday mornings.[23] More widows desire a comfortable life and good health than desire a close relationship with God. Widows tend to be patriotic, and actually respect the military as highly as the church.[24] While these attitudes in no way discredit the authenticity of widows' religious beliefs, it is worth noting that for this group Christianity is closely associated with patriotism and other civic virtues. Divorced people and never-marrieds with Christian beliefs do not share these associations as strongly as do widows and marrieds.

False Sense of Security?

After all the grim news in previous chapters, it is refreshing to hear that widows are optimistic about Christianity's future. American churches are meeting many widows' needs. Consequently, more than half consider the Christian faith relevant to the way they live.

Widows are often the church's loudest cheerleaders. About half of America's widows believe Christianity enjoys more influence on Americans today than it did five years ago. Widows consider the Protestant church sensitive not only to their needs but also to the needs of others, including young people.[25] In fact, those other groups tend to consider the church less sensitive to their needs, doubt that Christianity is experiencing a revival, and do not see traditional families coming back in style.

Good news? Yes, and no. These attitudes are welcome indicators that the church enjoys a good relationship with widows. But these attitudes also paint widows as somewhat out-of-touch with how Christianity is perceived outside the sanctuary. For instance, fewer than 40% of never-marrieds see Christianity as relevant to them. Only 20% see the local churches in their area as relevant to their needs.[26] Despite today's widows' praises for the church, tomorrow's elderly Americans are more likely to see and predict a post-Christian America.

Widows and the church enjoy an especially close relationship. In today's rapidly changing society, neither side can afford to take the other for granted. Tomorrow's widows will be different than today's. They may be less inclined toward tradition. They may be more comfortable with divorce and single parenthood. More may come from unchurched backgrounds. Tomorrow's churches will be different as well: more dominated by Baby Boomers, more concerned with younger Unmarried Americans, more ready to reconsider traditions that are more important to the church's supporters than they are to its mission fields.

Church culture is a mixed blessing. It tempts leaders to get comfortable, to concentrate on members' needs to the neglect of outsiders and to solicit advice only from insiders instead of other people who may see things in different ways. Cultural Christians can associate the Gospel with cultural values that Christians of other backgrounds may not share. They may miss opportunities to attract newcomers if their messages are geared toward other cultural Christians, to the exclusion of other groups. They could render themselves irrelevant to members of their communities who do not share their parishioners' ethnic backgrounds, cultures, needs or concerns. Conceivably they could send the wrong message to visitors who hear partisan prayers or sing "The Battle Hymn of the Republic" on Memorial Day.

And who are the most cultural of Christians? Widows and the elderly.

Churches who have the most effective ministries to widows tend to see widows the way some businesses see their most loyal customers and the way politicians see their most solid bases of support. These widowed adults are the very people James spoke of in the Scriptures. They are also the church's best workers and advertisers, and their accumulated wisdom is a tremendous resource that can be put to work educating and guiding younger generations.

But churches that are counting on their reputations to continue to reach and satisfy older Americans are in for a shock. It is feasible that the next generation of widows will arrive with a different agenda and culture. That "someday" is coming soon.

N O T E S

1 *Statistical Abstract of the United States 1992,* p. 43.

2 *Statistical Abstract of the United States 1992,* p. 42; and *Singleness in America.*

3 The Barna Research Group, Ltd., Family in America survey.

4 *Historical Statistics of the United States: Colonial Times to 1970,* p. 56.

5 Ibid., p. 224.

6 Ibid., p. 349.

7 U.S. Bureau of the Census, *Current Population Survey 1970-1988* (Washington, DC: U.S. Government Printing Office).

8 Statistical Abstract *of the United States 1992,* p. 44.

9 The Barna Research Group, Ltd., Family in America survey.

10 The Barna Research Group, Ltd., OmniPoll™ 2-91.

11 The Barna Research Group, Ltd., OmniPoll™ 1-91.

12 The Barna Research Group, Ltd., Family in America survey.

13 The Barna Research Group, Ltd., OmniPoll™ 1-91.

14 Ibid.

15 The Barna Research Group, Ltd., OmniPoll™ 2-91.

16 The Barna Research Group, Ltd., Family in America survey.

17 Ibid.

18 Ibid.

19 The Barna Research Group, Ltd., Family in America survey.

20 The Barna Research Group, Ltd., OmniPoll™ 1-91.

21 The Barna Research Group, Ltd., Family in America survey.

22 The Barna Research Group, Ltd., Family in America survey and OmniPoll™ 1-91.

23 The Barna Research Group, Ltd., OmniPoll™ 2-91.

24 The Barna Research Group, Ltd., OmniPoll™ 1-91.

25 The Barna Research Group, Ltd., OmniPoll™ 2-91.

26 The Barna Research Group, Ltd., OmniPoll™ 1-91.

C H A P T E R   E I G H T

What Happens Next?

We know much about the subgroups that comprise Unmarried America. As usual, there is good news and bad news. The question that naturally occurs is: What does the future hold?

Can we know what will happen to the American family, in all its forms, in the years and decades ahead? It is true that the world is too complex for much of the future to be even remotely predicted. Nevertheless, a look at the past can at least yield valuable hints at where to look for the forces that will shape the future.

The Role of the Economy

The preceding few chapters have outlined some of the demographic patterns that characterize Unmarried America. We have seen how change in America's economy has driven much of the change in American family structures in the twentieth century. A lot of social change resulted from freed labor, increased wealth, and new technology, both of which increased people's control over their own lives. In

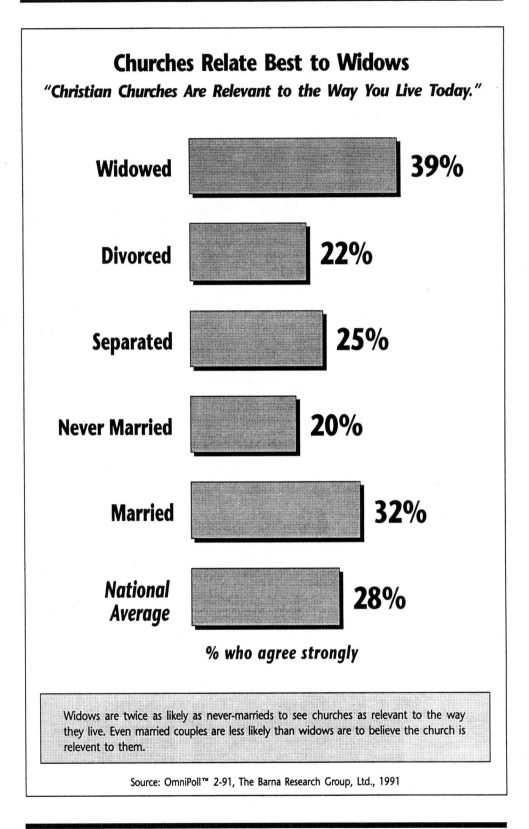

Churches Relate Best to Widows
"Christian Churches Are Relevant to the Way You Live Today."

Widowed — **39%**

Divorced — **22%**

Separated — **25%**

Never Married — **20%**

Married — **32%**

National Average — **28%**

% who agree strongly

Widows are twice as likely as never-marrieds to see churches as relevant to the way they live. Even married couples are less likely than widows are to believe the church is relevent to them.

Source: OmniPoll™ 2-91, The Barna Research Group, Ltd., 1991

the future, economic change will continue to drive social change within both Married and Unmarried America—often in unpredictable ways.

There is only one way for a nation like ours to grow richer on the whole, and that is to increase our worker productivity—the amount of money a person's hour of work produces. Since the early 1970's, American productivity has stagnated, experiencing only a modest revival in the mid-80's. This one economic fact is responsible for much of the despair among younger Americans as they assume that they will never be able to attain their parents' standard of living. It is also partly responsible for the trend toward two-earner families, as married couples seek to raise their income the only way they can: by working longer hours.

If American productivity begins to increase faster than it has in the last twenty years, the mood in America will brighten considerably, especially among younger wage-earners. But there is every reason to expect instead that the economic costs of regulation on business and the heavy load of America's growing national debt will continue to slow productivity growth and burden American workers. Singles and especially single parents will be affected more than married couples and families, since their costs of living are proportionately higher than their incomes.

Assuming an anemic economy in the near future, what social changes might we see that involve those inside and outside marriages?

What the Future Holds

So many unpredictable forces will play a part in shaping America that the only truly safe prediction is that things will change. Nevertheless, a few predictions help describe what life in tomorrow's Unmarried America is likely to be like, barring too many unforeseen circumstances:

- *Marriage will continue to lose its former hold on social status.* Younger generations will grow more conservative as they age, but they will be replaced by generations with values that are even less traditional than their own. The move away from traditional values exploded with the Baby Boomers, and continues among Baby Busters. There is no end, much less reversal, in sight.

- *Cohabitation will grow in public acceptance.* Baby Busters are a generation that is particularly comfortable with the idea of cohabitation. Even if they are somewhat uncomfortable with the practice themselves, they are tolerant of cohabiting by others. Cohabitation's social stigma is declining rapidly among young Americans. America will probably follow much of Europe's lead in accepting cohabitation.

- *Widows will exhibit declining traditionalism.* As never-married and divorced people join widows and married couples in higher age groups, the diversity of lifestyles, values and attitudes within that age cohort will grow. Older unmarried Americans, and especially elderly couples and widows, will always be more traditional than other Americans; but the gap between them will shrink.

- *Growth rates for single parenthood and divorced single parenthood will level off, but at rates higher than they are today.* Divorce rates have already begun to stabilize in the last few years. At some point, family deterioration will stabilize as well, though at a higher rate than today's.

  Single parenthood among blacks is leveling off simply because it cannot go much higher.[1] Single parenthood among whites and hispanics is still a minority family arrangement, so it has a lot more room to rise. But it is unlikely to reach the level realized among black Americans any time soon.

- *Single parenthood and divorced life will never be glamorous.* The economic hardships that single parenthood and divorce cause will keep these lifestyles from being socially attractive, despite their increased acceptability. This will in turn influence behavior in powerful and lasting, but different and even opposing, directions. (For instance, fear of single parenthood increases abstinence, marriage, contraception use and abortion simultaneously. Likewise, fear of divorce produces stable marriages, but also people who never marry and who live together.)

- *Young Americans will grow increasingly comfortable with sex outside marriage.* The incredible prevalence of sex on television and in nearly every other aspect of American life has broken down the traditional association of sex restricted to marriage. (As film critic Michael Medved has asked, how often do movies portray sex scenes between happily married adults?) Fear of disease and pregnancy are only weak brakes on teens', much less adults', sexual behaviors. Morality hardly has the power it once enjoyed.[2] Nevertheless, a small but steady minority of Americans will continue to abstain from sex until marriage.

- *Fertility will continue to decline.* The cost of raising children, the growing tendency to delay marriage and delay childbearing as well, and the availability of contraception and abortion all helped bring fertility down to below "replacement level" (slightly above two children per woman) in 1990. Some demographers predict that only a minority of today's young women will have more than one child, and that up to one-quarter will have no children at all.[3]

- *Stable marriages and nuclear families will become elite lifestyles.* Many forces will combine to make this happen: the economies of scale that married couples experience, the wealth-generating ability of dual-earner professional couples, declining family sizes and nuclear families' ability to save money and own their homes. Even as married couples with children decline in proportion to the American population, their relative wealth will increase dramatically.

  In a recent article, *Money* magazine's highest recommendation for young Americans who want to be wealthy was simply to wait until marriage to have children. Traditional families will enjoy a growing economic advantage over the alternatives.

- *American society will stratify between traditional and nontraditional families.* Traditional families are more likely to educate their children well, to produce more wealth for inheritance and to pass on traditions that lead those children into traditional families themselves. It is possible to foresee a future where single parents live primarily in neighborhoods with enormous infrastructure problems, large welfare burdens and restricted job opportunities, while married families will live in neighborhoods with more residential housing, healthier economies, higher tax bases, safer streets and stronger institutions, including schools. This trend, already developing, will continue to worsen economic inequality.

- *Traditional families will communicate traditions and religion to children more effectively than others.* Another force dividing traditional and non-traditional families will be the relative ease with which traditional families can pass along traditions to their young. Children of stable families will be better educated and possess stronger family values. Since church attendance rises with marriage and parenthood, children of traditional families will continue to be more likely to be churched than those whose parents are never-married or divorced. They may be more religious as well. On the other hand, the group of Americans who grow up and live lives entirely outside Christian churches will grow quickly.

- *If society stratifies between traditional families and alternative families, churches will tend to stratify along the same lines.* Churches already tend to draw along cultural lines. If marital boundaries increasingly define cultural boundaries, they will increasingly define religious boundaries and church cultures as well. We may see "traditional" churches with traditional-family oriented congregations and traditional-family theologies, and "alternative" churches with congregations holding different family values. These churches' budgets, spending priorities and outreach priorities will tend to reflect the interests of their congregations (as they always have).

    This is not a radical new trend so much as it is a continued trend within the Church which will simply be responding to the new social forces unleashed by the changing American family.

- *Various ethnic groups will experience these social changes differently.* Ethnic groups show stark differences from each other in their marriage, divorce and single parenthood rates. Cultures influence the way people respond to the forces in their lives. Ethnic cultures with stronger family structures and values—some Central and East Asian subcultures, for example—will weather economic and social change better than those without. They will find upward mobility easier and faster, and may assimilate with more of their native culture intact. How assimilation into the American mainstream affects the family cultures of recent immigrants is a developing story that is worth watching.

- *Traditional families will benefit from the Information Age.* Two-parent families, with their greater prosperity and greater educational achievements, will be especially well suited to an information-based economy. If America continues the current shift toward an information-rich, service-based labor force, expect traditional families to be the biggest beneficiaries and single-parent households and their children to be at an economic and educational disadvantage.

- *Unmarried America and Married America will diverge politically.* Since these two groups will increasingly have different economic interests, they will have different taxation, government spending and transfer payment interests as well. Traditional families will tend to push for middle-class spending patterns: low tax rates; tax deductions for mortgage interest, dependents and children; spending on the local level rather than the state or federal level; law enforcement and defense; and "middle-class welfare" like Social Security. Unmarrieds, on the other hand, will prefer spending that reflects their own interests: higher top tax rates; job-training and welfare; national health insurance (since their employment tends to be less stable); and day-care and pregnancy benefits for single mothers.

  Expect these divergent political attitudes to be played out *within* the Democratic and Republic parties as well as *between* them. The fact that half of all Americans are expected to be unmarried by the year 2000 means that an exclusively "family" party would by necessity be a minority party. On the other hand, the "family" vote will be a powerful, wealthy voting bloc to be reckoned with.[4] Therefore, both parties will need to attract the votes of unmarrieds—without alienating their powerful family contingents—in order to win majorities. On balance, this probably bodes well for platforms and candidates that avoid alienating either group. It does not bode well for policies (including anti-abortion policies) that are especially unpopular with one group or the other.

- *Churches' teachings and theologies relating to marriage, family and divorce will develop and change.* Church history shows that Christians tend to develop creeds, statements of faith and attitudes in response to the battles and challenges they are experiencing. The next few decades will see churches develop their theologies more precisely in the family area, as they seek to apply biblical and church teachings to the diverse needs and experiences of Unmarried Americans. Increased attention to abortion and school prayer in response to Supreme Court decisions are good examples of developing theological family issues. Stands on family issues may grow in prominence in churches' belief statements. Approaches may well diverge into two main camps: "traditionalists," whose theology resists demographic and lifestyle changes, and "progressives," who theologically accommodate Unmarried America's changing values in relation to issues like cohabitation, divorce, sex outside of marriage, abortion and single parenthood. Churches whose congregations are predominantly married will not necessarily be traditionalists, and churches whose congregations are mostly unmarried will not necessarily be progressives. Divorced people's views on marriage, for instance, are unusually traditional. And the black church has always fought family breakdown in its communities. On the other hand, many liberal churches have upscale, suburban congregations with lots of intact families. They thrive on challenging prevailing attitudes, rather than accommodating them. Neither chasing trends nor fighting them is a guaranteed strategy for success.

The scope of change over the next few decades will be breathtaking. Some of Unmarried America's attitudes—widespread rejection of the idea that sex is only proper within marriage, the increased acceptability of cohabitation, the growing prevalence of single parenthood—are unprecedented in their magnitude. Powerful currents of change exist alongside powerful currents of tradition. That these changes will affect the most basic of our institutions, the family, is especially unsettling. Yet most people will continue to experience marriage, parenthood and old age, all of which tend to make people more interested in God—and also tend to lull some ministries into complacency.

What, then, should churches do to serve the needs of Unmarried America without compromising their beliefs and values?

N   O   T   E   S

1   U.S. Bureau of the Census data, cited in *The American Enterprise*, March/April 1991.

2   Popenoe, p. 19.

3   Ibid.

4   Barnes, Fred, "The Family Gap: A Readers' Digest Poll," *Readers' Digest* (July 1992), pp. 48-52.

C H A P T E R   N I N E

How Should the Church Respond?

A look at the divergent groups of Unmarried America is enough to induce panic in some quarters. Is America out of control? Will we become separate societies with a shared geography? Is premarital sex now a given? Will childhood in a "traditional family" be a privilege for only an elite few? Will the message of Christianity be lost amidst all the other messages? How can one church possibly serve all the needs that will be arising?

Is the Narrow Gate Really the Best?

Many ministries cannot adequately serve the plethora of needs that will emerge. Therefore they target a group, or series of groups, and focus primarily on their needs—in the process becoming much more effective ministries. For instance, Roman Catholic churches are becoming legendary for providing effective but inexpensive education for inner-city youth. They now advertise their school systems in newspapers, on billboards and even over the airwaves. Prison Fellowship reaches out to America's growing incarcerated population. Numerous rescue missions target America's down-and-out. Young Life targets high school kids and Campus Crusade largely targets college students. The examples of outstanding niche ministries are endless. And it is interesting that the success of these ministries is not necessarily due to their ability to be on the same cultural wavelength as their target market, but to excel in performing a much-needed service to their communities.

"Narrowcasting," the practice of targeting a message toward one particular group, has its limits when the targets are as diverse as the subgroups of Unmarried America. People whose lives do not quite fit the model may not find the targeted message compelling. They may even resent being categorized and stereotyped.

Many churches narrowcast by splitting groups up and working individually with each. But groups that are apart from each other can no longer interact. Groups that are cloistered miss a great educational opportunity: that of enjoying and learning from others who are different. In many American schools and churches, young people are left to work out their worldviews in the absence of people with more experience and usually more wisdom. As George Santayana might have said (had he not been an atheist), "Those Sunday schoolers who cannot remember the past are condemned to repeat it."

But narrowcasting has strengths as well as weaknesses. Unmarried America's subgroups share fundamental commonalities that are worth working with. Never-marrieds share some common experiences which are not the common experiences shared by widows. Every divorced person has lived through a traumatic experience that has left profound effects on his or her life and has created needs in common with many other divorced adults. Social, economic and demographic forces unify Unmarried America's subgroups in important ways. Narrowcasting can be an efficient and effective way to respond to the effects of those forces. It is also a proven means of capturing the attention of the people for whom the communication or event was intended. In a marketplace cluttered with broad-based, unfocused, irrelevant messages, targeting a group through highly focused language, concepts, and activities can work wonders.

Careful with that Sledgehammer

It is up to individual churches to design creative approaches that will attract Unmarried Americans, serve their needs and allow opportunities for them to contribute to the work of the church in their own ways. Questions like when to broadcast and when to narrowcast, or whether one service can speak to everyone at once, have to be answered one church at a time—and only after careful and thorough study. And some caution is in order before churches set out to reach groups as complex as these. Demographic research is a valuable but rather blunt instrument. The categories of unmarrieds hide similarities among groups as well as masking differences within them. For example, elderly divorcees act much like widows. Never-married and divorced parents share similar values with married parents. And some divorced people, particularly men, behave much like never-marrieds.

Indeed, a group's statistics often fail to show the true diversity resident within the membership of the group. A danger in interpreting statistics is in thinking that people actually fit into the neat categories demographers work with. They do not. The generalizing that makes it possible to examine the broad trends common to groups of people also makes it easy to ignore the differences among them. There are plenty of traditional never-marrieds and lots of radical widows. Even the narrowest of demographic slices still contains a wide variety of people.

For instance, demographers speak of "whites," "blacks" and "hispanics" as if they were all of one mind. But people of different ethnicities share profoundly different values. Blacks disapprove more than whites of cohabitation as an alternative to marriage, but support it more than whites as a prelude to marriage. Hispanics feel stronger marriage ties than other ethnics. Asians—a group neglected until recently by many studies because of their comparatively small numbers—look much like whites in their marital stability, but tend to form extended families rather than nuclear families. And these broad racial groupings hide the uniqueness of the myriad cultural backgrounds within each.

Race is just one of the factors demographers use to slice up America. Urbanites have their own set of attitudes, while people who live in the country have another. Highly educated unmarrieds have untraditional views of marriage, family and religion. Age—especially the lack of it—has a huge effect on attitude and lifestyle. Income has another huge effect. And the difference between men and women on some issues is legendary.

Think again about the images of "singles" that you are most familiar with. How do they square with the reality of Unmarried America and the character of *your* community?

Here is a common television image: young, white, never-married men and women living glamorous, independent lives and radiating "coolness." Some are college graduates beginning their long climb up the ladder of success while fighting a cruel economy—a sort of nineties' version of yuppiehood. Others hang out on city streets in their torn jeans and blazing white athletic shoes—the recessionary middle class. Dating preoccupies all; marriage preoccupies none. They switch between fashionable apathy and fashionable activism on the environment, the economy and other issues of the day. The world's troubles occasionally haunt them: economic stagnation, crime, AIDS, existential emptiness. But most of the time they seem to be enjoying their brave new world.

This is the picture on TV, on movie billboards and in commercials. It is probably not a perfect match with your a community. Nationwide, the reality is infinitely richer than the image. It brims with sexual, ethnic, educational, economic and cultural differences. Think about the individuals the stereotype ignores. What about *older* people who never married? What about the single parents we hear about? One does not see *them* in jeans commercials. What about life in middle-class suburbia? in inner cities? in the country? No research report is likely to describe all of the nuances of individual lives in our nation, let alone your particular community.

Difficult, But Worth It

These pages have sketched only silhouettes of Unmarried America. Churches will find the information useful in beginning to understand how the American family is evolving in the last years of this century and in seeing how truly different from its former self America has become.

But churches will need to do their own research to uncover the profiles of the people of their communities and to understand those people's unique needs and values. It is here that our common study ends and the customized detective work begins. Sociological research of this nature, even on a local level, can be complicated and expensive. But it is crucial. Much will be found that is in common with the Unmarried America portrayed here; but many important differences will likely be uncovered as well. They will need to be taken into account in order for ministry strategies to achieve maximum success.

America is changing before our eyes, in ways we are only beginning to understand. Ignoring the changes will only take churches out of the picture. Responding to inaccurate information or invalid assumptions will only waste precious time and resources, while reinforcing the perception that churches are irrelevant or out of touch.

A pastor who visits churches throughout America came back to visit his former church. He bore this message: If the church does not get to work, its children will never know the America their parents grew up with and loved.

He was half right. The America we know today will not exist in twenty years. Neither will its families, its communities, its economy, or its churches. Neither turning back the clock nor stopping it are options.

However, churches have the opportunity to play a role in shaping the America that *does exist* in twenty years. Their role in the lives of tomorrow's never-marrieds, divorced people, widows, married couples and children is, in part, up to them.

Barna Research Group, Ltd.

Dedicated to the Needs of the Christian Community

Begun in 1984 by George and Nancy Barna, Barna Research Group, Ltd. has become the nation's largest full-service marketing research company dedicated to the needs of the Christian community. To provide cost-efficient and timely information, the company uses sophisticated data collection systems to evaluate current conditions and track emerging trends.

Our goal is to serve Christ by keeping the Church well-informed about the society in which we have been called to minister. That means providing information about the changing face of American society while remaining sensitive to the special calling of the Church in a market-driven economy.

In addition to the reports, books, and audio tapes described here, Barna Research offers syndicated studies of specialized markets; community and congregational studies for churches; seminars and public presentations; and custom research studies for organizations.

Answers to Questions People Frequently Ask Us

↪ We are an independent, privately-owned, for-profit organization. In addition to working with churches and parachurch ministries, we conduct research for secular clients such as advertising agencies, television networks, and financial institutions. We subsist by charging clients fees for the projects and products we provide.

↪ Each of the reports we develop is based on original, primary research which we fund independently. As a general rule, each report contains information that costs us in excess of $10,000 to collect. By charging a minimal user fee for the information and analysis, we attempt to recoup as much of our investment as possible.

Resources from the Barna Research Group, Ltd.

Today's Pastors
Book (by George Barna), Published 1993

This ground-breaking study of more than 1000 Protestant senior pastors describes what pastors are thinking about ministry, the laity, the local church and about themselves as leaders. The book includes the latest church statistics, ranging from attendance figures to conversions to pastoral compensation packages. Chapters on leadership preparation and addressing congregational expectations provide additional practical help.

There may be no tougher job in America than pastoring a church—and the data underscore just how difficult and taxing the job is for most pastors. Obtain insights into what does and does not work for pastors, and why the Church is struggling to have an impact on American society.

Absolute Confusion
Book (by George Barna), Published 1993

This is the third annual Barna Report exploring a wide variety of beliefs, values and attitudes among the adult population. This year's version looks at issues such as racial tension, homosexuality, media influence and objectivity, family values, morality, political ideology and media usage. There are three chapters which update trends related to people's religious beliefs and practices. You'll learn about changes in church attendance patterns, beliefs about God, involvement in small groups, prayer, and perceptions of the Christian faith.

The title refers to the inescapable dichotomy between what we say and what we do: we are a nation of people absolutely confused about what is true and what is contrived. And while Americans are searching for answers, we show little evidence of moving back toward Biblical truth.

The Future of the American Family
Book (by George Barna), Published 1993

Here's the latest on the state of the family in America. With data culled from special Barna studies, as well as work from other leading researchers, find out what's happening concerning family attitudes and behavior. Discover a dozen widely-held misperceptions about the family of the nineties. Read about the trends in family practices and desires.

In some ways, the family is not as bad off as you've been led to believe, but in other ways matters are definitely getting worse. All this information is contained in chapters that focus upon current trends regarding our definitions of family; marriage; divorce; singles; homosexuality; minority families; family time and activities; faith and the family; and steps toward strengthening the family unit.

Turnaround Churches
Book (by George Barna), Published 1993

There are thousands of churches in this country that are stagnant or declining—and a relative handful who break free from that condition to begin growing again. Through extensive interviews with turnaround pastors, this book reveals the keys to a successful church turnaround.

For pastors of churches which are currently healthy, the book provides insight into how to avoid entering the downward spiral.

The Invisible Generation: Baby Busters
Book (by George Barna), Published 1992

There are many resources available concerning Baby Boomers and Senior Citizens. But what about the generation now coming of age: the Baby Busters? What do you know about them?

The Busters represent the second-largest generation in the nation's history, yet most people have ignored their existence, focusing instead upon the Boomers. Are you prepared to minister to the ascending adult population? In *The Invisible Generation: Baby Busters,* find out who these people are, and how to strategically develop your ministry to penetrate this important population group.

In this groundbreaking analysis of the post-Boomer generation, George Barna provides a comprehensive examination of the new generation.

Among the topics explored are the demographics of the generation; how they differ from previous generations; their expectations; the values, morals, and perspectives that shape their lives; their lifestyles and personal relationships; their spiritual beliefs, attitudes and activities; and their views on family and work.

The Power of Vision: How You Can Capture and Apply God's Vision for Your Ministry
Revised edition of Without a Vision, the People Perish, by George Barna, Published 1992

Grasping God's vision for your church's ministry is not optional. To minister authentically and authoritatively you must determine, embrace, cast, and implement that vision. It should become the focus of your life's work and the heartbeat of your church. In this book, you'll learn the practical realities of how to empower your ministry through discovering and living His vision.

A Step-by-Step Guide to Church Marketing: Breaking Ground for the Harvest
Book (by George Barna), Published 1992

Church Marketing is the long-awaited companion workbook to George Barna's seminal work, *Marketing the Church.* In this hands-on, application-oriented guide book, Barna gives feet to the principles discussed in *Marketing the Church,* and takes leaders on a step-by-step process of discovery and application.

If you have been hindered in your desire to help your church collect relevant information; interpret data about your audience; clarify God's vision for the ministry; grasp a strategic view of your ministry; put together a ministry marketing plan; or determine how to most effectively communicate with a target population—then this is the resource you've been waiting for.

The Barna Report '92-93: America Renews Its Search for God
Book (by George Barna), Published 1992

Are people's attitudes changing? What about their beliefs and religious behavior? In an era of rapid change and social turbulence, what are the latest insights needed to understand and minister to the American people?

In The *Barna Report 1992-93,* George Barna continues the annual *Barna Report* series, exploring a wide range of important topics and issues. Following the format of last year's *What Americans Believe,* the new release provides a useful blend of commentary, visuals and data tables to unfold a revealing look at who we are and where we are headed as a nation.

User Friendly Churches: What Christians Need to Know About Churches People Love to Attend
Book (by George Barna), Published 1991

Why reinvent the wheel? Instead, learn from the experiences of other churches, and build on what has led to their success. This book was designed to shorten your learning curve by describing what a diverse group of churches from across the nation have in common that is causing growth, both numerically and in the personal spiritual lives of their people.

In *User Friendly Churches,* investigate the 10 attributes many churches exhibit—but which were absent in the activity of the growing congregations we studied. In addition, see how the attitude of these user friendly churches differed from the norm. Learn the key questions to ask if your church is serious about growth, and decide which aspects of ministry should and should not be challenged.

What Americans Believe: An Annual Survey of Values and Religious Views in the United States
Book (by George Barna), Published 1991

In *What Americans Believe* you'll find out about American values, lifestyles, religious beliefs, attitudes, and relationships. A wealth of information is presented in a user friendly format, including easy-to-read charts and data tables. For each survey question asked, we include a brief analysis to help you make the most of the information. This book will reshape your perceptions and keep you in touch with what Americans believe today.

The Frog in the Kettle: What Christians Need to Know About Life in the Year 2000
Book (by George Barna), Published 1990

Because we are immersed in a changing environment, we often fail to perceive the shifts taking place around us. Yet, each time the Church fails to perceive and respond to such change, it loses ground in the unfolding spiritual battle. This book offers a road map to guide you through the chaos ahead, and to make a discernible difference in the restructuring of America.

Understand why the Nineties are the make-it-or-break-it decade for the Christian Church while exploring the new values of Americans, and why those values require a new orientation in ministry. See how and why a new form of religion will replace Christianity as America's dominant faith, and what that faith will be like.

Ten Years Later: Personal Lessons from a Decade of Research and Ministry
Book (by George Barna), Published 1992

Have you ever sat back and reflected on the specific lessons you've learned about people, organizations, society, and yourself over the past decade? It can be a challenging and revealing practice.

In *Ten Years Later,* George Barna provides some personal reflections on what he has discovered about the world he studies. This book contains some of the more striking insights he has gleaned from a decade of research, teaching, and participation in both Christian ministry and in the "secular" marketplace. Having had a foot in two unique worlds—working with major international corporations as well as Christian churches and parachurch ministries—Barna details some of the lessons that these experiences have taught him on a variety of fronts.

The Mind of the Donor
Research Report, Published 1994

If you want to understand more about why Americans give money to non-profit and charitable organizations, this report provides novel insights. Based upon a new study of giving habits and motivations, the report provides a unique typology of donors—and discusses marketing strategies that correspond with each donor segment.

Americans give away more money than any other people in the world—by a long shot. But the giving patterns associated with our contributions are changing radically as new values take root and as the Boomers and Busters ascend to center stage in the donor arena. If your organization relies upon people's generosity, use this report to discover what's going on in the minds and lives of the donor base.

Unmarried America
Research Report, Published 1993

This report offers new information regarding the singles population and related ministry opportunities. The report divides the unmarried population into its three component parts—the never-been-marrieds, the divorced and the widowed—and differentiates their values, beliefs, behavior and expectations for the future.

Those who believe that all single adults are alike and can be effectively ministered to through a one-size-fits-all singles ministry will be surprised by many of the findings. The three singles segments are significantly different in their views on life, people and ministry. Outreach to this growing population ought to reflect the distinctive qualities of each singles segment.

Never on a Sunday: The Challenge of the Unchurched
Research Report, Published 1990

Most church growth is transfer growth—circulating the saints from one congregation to another. Meanwhile, the proportion of unchurched adults continues to grow, virtually untapped. Why? Because we have failed to understand who they are and what they respond to. Here are many insights that will enhance your outreach efforts.

From this resource, find out which population groups are most likely to be unchurched and why the unchurched have made a conscious decision to reject the Church; explore the religious beliefs and activities of these people; and find out that they are *not* isolated from religious endeavors. Most importantly, see why you need a well-conceived plan to reach the unchurched—not just good intentions and a simplistic outreach program.

Today's Teens: A Generation in Transition
Research Report, Published 1991

Kids aged 13-18 are at the heart of the Baby Bust—the generation that is usurping the role of the Baby Boomers as the major change agents in America. They also represent your best prospects for evangelism. But what do you really know about them?

Today's Teens examines the underlying values and attitudes that drive teens' behavior, and asks who influences teenagers the most—and the least. Find out the most pressing concerns and needs teens feel, what their dreams are for the future—and how those dreams influence their behavior and attitudes. We also examine the role of music in the lifestyle of teens—and what role it could play in ministry to them. Most importantly, learn why ministry to teens holds perhaps the greatest potential for the future of the Church.

Sources of Information for Ministry and Business
Research Report, Updated & Revised in 1992

This report catalogues specific sources of information needed for ministry and social/market analysis. Included are books published in the last five years that will be of value to church leaders striving to understand the new America; government data bases available for your use—many at no cost—which often go untapped; and other media—magazines, newsletters, audio tapes, video tapes—which would benefit your ministry.

In addition to the more common media, *Sources* also identifies two dozen special reports recently produced which provide insights directly relevant to Christian ministry. It also discusses the use of on-line data bases that provide instant access to nationwide surveys and other data banks.

The User Friendly Inventory

Have you ever wondered how your church stacks up against the user friendly churches of America? Here is a 100-item evaluation tool to help you explore the heartbeat and performance of your church in light of George Barna's research on what makes a growing, spiritually powerful church tick. Packaged in sets of five, this inventory has been an eye-opening tool to help staff and lay leaders more objectively assess what their church is really like, and to focus on what's truly important in ministry. As a discussion-starter or performance yardstick, let The User Friendly Inventory help you refine and refocus your ministry.

The Audio Series from Barna Research:
'Creating a User Friendly Church' & 'Current Trends'

In the first two sessions of this audio series, hear George Barna describe the trends that are radically transforming the ways in which we minister effectively today. In "Current Trends," Barna describes the current and likely future conditions related to demographics, values, lifestyles, the family, and religion. "Creating a User Friendly Church" describes the 15 principles that Barna's research discovered as the basis for churches that were coping successfully with societal change.

Each tape comes with a notebook that contains an outline of Barna's presentation, plus critical questions for your consideration, and suggested sources for additional information. These aides were designed to help you discern the implications of Barna's research for your church, toward enhancing your ministry.

Church Growth Without Compromise Seminars for Church Leaders:
Understanding Ministry in a Changing Culture

Join George Barna for two days of intensive teaching geared to help you clarify mission, vision, values, trends, and strategies related to your ministry. If you're willing to take an honest look at your church, and to take an extensive look at our society and your opportunities in ministry, this seminar will provide you with invaluable insight and perspective.

Is your church user friendly? Vision-driven? Strategically positioned? Come and explore these and other dimensions of your ministry.